Colwinston Church, Glamorgan

THE OLD PARISH CHURCHES

OF GWENT,

GLAMORGAN & GOWER

Mike Salter

FOLLY PUBLICATIONS

ACKNOWLEDGEMENTS

The photographs in this book were taken by the author, who also drew the map and the plans and sketches. A few old postcards are also reproduced from the author's collection. Thanks are due to Helen Thomas for driving on most of the recent trips to take fresh photos and re-examine many of the buildings for this second edition.

ABOUT THIS BOOK

As with the other churches books in this series (see full list inside back cover) this book concentrates on the period before the Industrial Revolution and the subsequent dramatic population increase necessitated the construction of many new churches to serve the expanding urban areas. Most furnishings and monuments after 1800 are not mentioned in this book, although additions and alterations to older churches are. Churches founded after 1800 are not mentioned in the gazetteers, except in one or two cases where new churches superseded older ones nearby or on different sites.

The title used for the original 1991 edition of this book has been retained despite the fact that the name Monmouthshire has been reinstated for most of the area then known as Gwent. The book basically covers the pre-1974 counties of Monmouthshire and Glamorgan but with Gower divided off with its own gazetteer, partly because it was a separate lordship in medieval times, and partly for visitors to the Gower peninsular needing material on the churches there conveniently grouped together.

This book is very much a catalogue of descriptions, dates and names. It is intended as a field guide and for reference rather than to be read from cover to cover. Sometimes there are comments about the settings of churches but on the whole lack of space has permitted few comments about their position or atmosphere. Occasionally the most interesting features of a church or graveyard may lie outside the scope of this book as outlined above, or the setting of a building may be more exciting than its features. The gazetteers include Ordnance Survey grid references (these are the two letters and six digits which appear after each place-name and dedication) and is intended to be used in conjunction with O.S. 1:50,000 scale maps. These are vital for finding churches in remote areas or amongst urban sprawl.

Plans redrawn from the author's field notes are reproduced to a common scale of 1:400. The buildings were measured in metres and only metric scales are given. For those who feel a need to convert to imperial scales three metres is almost ten feet. A system of hatching common to all the church plans in the books in this series is used to denote the different periods of work. On some pages there is insufficient space for a key to be shown. If so, simply refer to another page. The plans shown be treated with some caution. Some features are difficult to date and others are not easy to depict on small scale drawings, such as dressed (cut) stones of one period being later reused either in situ or moved to another part of the building.

ABOUT THE AUTHOR

Mike Salter is 49 and has been a professional author-publisher since he went on the Government Enterprise Allowance Scheme for unemployed people in 1988. He is particularly interested in the planning and layout of medieval buildings and has a huge collection of plans of churches and castles he has measured during tours (mostly be bicycle and motorcycle) of all parts of the British Isles since 1968. Wolverhampton born and bred, Mike now lives in an old cottage beside the Malvern Hills. His other interests include walking, maps, railways, board games, morris dancing, playing percussion instruments and calling folk dances with a ceilidh band.

Copyright 1991 & 2002 by Mike Salter. This second edition published Dec 2002.
Folly Publications, Folly Cottage, 151 West Malvern Rd, Malvern, Worcs WR14 4AY
Printed by Aspect Design, 89 Newtown Road, Malvern, Worcs, WR14 2PD

St Brides Wentloog Church

CONTENTS

Maps of the churches described appear inside the front cover

INTRODUCTION

Christianity existed in Wales during the Roman period but little remains of any churches earlier than the Norman invasion of the 1090s, although there are fine collections of early crosses and memorial slabs at Llantwit Major and Margam. By the 9th century there were many monastic mother churches (clas), each administering several small chapels-of-ease. The chapels were probably wood or unmortared stone, but it is assumed that the mother churches were of mortared stone with small round-arched openings and thatched roofs. Nothing now stands of their walls, although traces of an early stone church on the site of a still earlier wooden church were revealed in an excavation at Llanbad aimed at looking for Arthurian period remains.

By 1100 the Normans had founded Benedictine priories at Monmouth, Chepstow, Cardiff and Abergavenny, and others followed at Ewenny (c1140) and Usk (c1175). These establishments erected stone churches on a much grander scale than anything previously seen in Wales. Ruination or rebuilding has removed much of the early work but Chepstow retains the arcades of an early aisled nave, Usk a central tower of c1180, Ewenny an almost complete cruciform 12th century church, and one wide arch remains at Llandaff Cathedral. Townsfolk usually worshiped in the western parts of these monastic churches and ensured that some parts of them survived after the monasteries were dissolved by Henry VIII in the late 1530s. However the monastic church at Cardiff was later completely lost as a result of river erosion. Of the rather more modest early 12th century village churches there remain plain narrow doorways at Portskewitt and St Hilary, walling with herringbone masonry at Dixton and Old Cogan and also a nave at Llandegfedd.

Norman arch in Newport Cathedral

Chancel Arch at Runton

Herringbone masonry at Old Cogan

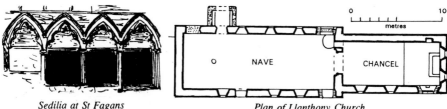

Sedilia at St Fagans   *Plan of Llanthony Church*

From c1150 to 1200 there was a boom in church building. Almost all the churches then existing were rebuilt or extended and many new churches were founded, quite a lot of them in conjunction with nearby castles. More than a tenth of the 230 medieval churches in Gwent and Glamorgan either retain a central core (usually part of the nave) of this period, or they have a window or doorway either in situ or removed elsewhere, or they have an early tub font. The ruin at Runston illustrates a typical small church or chapel of this period. The congregation would have stood on a rush-covered earth floor in a rectangular nave with a thatched roof and whitewashed internal walls decorated with simple motifs painted mostly in red, yellow or black. Later these developed into murals of scenes from the lives of Christ and the saints. On each of the north and south sides was a doorway and a tiny window, all of them round arched like the chancel arch, through which the congregation could see into the chancel. The latter was a square room lighted with two or three windows and was just large enough to contain the altar and an attendant priest. The arcades remain of aisled 12th century naves at Newport and Margam, the latter a Cistercian abbey later taken over as a parish church. Several churches have late 12th century towers but in every case the original belfry windows have been replaced by later remodelling or rebuilding.

Although monastic churches usually had aisled naves, in Wales it was not very common for the medieval congregations of purely parochial churches to increase sufficiently to warrant enlarging the nave by adding on an aisle or two. In Gwent the churches serving nearby castles at Skenfrith, Grosmont and Llantilio Crosseny all had aisles on either side by c1300, as did Mathern, which served the bishop of Llandaff's palace, and Trelleck, a planted town rebuilt in the 1290s. Caerwent and nearby Christchurch also had at least one 13th century aisle. Mitchel Troy has 14th century aisles and there are others of the 15th century at Magor, Peterstone Wentloog, Redwick and a few other places, but the majority of the churches still remain without aisles. They are still rarer in Glamorgan, although Llancarfan had an aisle by c1200, Coychurch and Llantwit Major have pairs of fairly narrow late 13th century aisles, and there are late medieval aisles at Cardiff, St Andrews Major, and Cowbridge, the latter a replacement of a chapel-of-ease elsewhere in the parish.

Towers, on the other hand, are common in South Wales churches. By the 1540s over two thirds of the churches of Gwent and Glamorgan possessed something more substantial to hang bells in than a simple bellcote on the west wall, and an even higher proportion had a stone porch in front of the main doorway. The towers mostly lie at the west end of the nave but about a dozen or so lie in a central position between the nave and chancel, in addition to the monastic churches where this was normal. Some of the central towers were accompanied by transepts. Llanblethian is an instance of where a transept was provided without a central tower. Transepts provided space for subsidiary altars and often also contained niches for tombs of benefactors. In the rare instances of a tower lying in a transeptal position, as at Ilston and St Mellons, the lowest storey formed a chapel with an altar. Medieval vestries are rare but examples survive at Cowbridge, Llantwit Major, Llysworney and Trelleck.

The building boom begun c1150 slowed down in the early 14th century, and the ravages of the plague finally brought most new work to a halt c1350. In the 1190s the pointed arch began to appear in chancel arches and was gradually also adopted for arcades, windows and doorways. More than half of the churches of Gwent and Glamorgan have 13th century masonry or openings. Most of the work is minor, difficult to date accurately, or has subsequently been altered or restored. In Gwent only the unaisled churches of Marshfield and Michaelston-y-Fedw, and the aisled buildings at Grosmont and Skenfrith are of importance. Of note in Glamorgan (including Gower) are Cheriton, Cowbridge, Coychurch, Llantwit Major, and Llysworney, all of which have central towers. Chancels of the this period usually have a separate doorway and are larger than before since the use of choirs (which needed more space) was gradually coming into fashion in the larger parish churches.

By the end of the late 13th century the single pointed-headed lancet lights used from c1200 onwards were sometimes given cusped heads and placed together in pairs. Eventually the spandrel between their heads would be pierced, as at Llangwm Uchaf, Llantwit Major and Llanvapley, and so tracery evolved. The elaborate floral and geometrical tracery designs typical of parish churches in many parts of England c1290-1360 are rarely seen in Wales apart from in major monastic churches like Tintern Abbey. In the aisled naves at Trelleck and Mitchel Troy, the south aisle and chapel at Llancarfan, and in the new Gower churches of Rhossili, Pennard and Penmaen (which all replaced Norman churches engulfed by sand-dunes) window tracery is either kept very simple or is absent altogether. Slightly more ambitious windows can be seen in the cruciform churches at Coity and St Georges in Glamorgan. There are spires of medieval origin (even if rebuilt) at Trelleck and Grosmont, something of a rarity in South Wales.

Churchyard cross
at St Donat's

Llancarfan Church

Raglan Church

Dating of architectural features in Wales can be problematical, where few records have survived and where new ideas were sometimes slow to be adopted and then were retained for decades after they fell out of fashion in England. Several churches have a window or two which are perhaps late 14th century insertions. A larger number have a features likely to indicate some remodelling in the period 1400 to c1470, but there was not much completely new construction. New foundations only now occurred when an older site nearby was threatened by the elements, as at Pyle, which replaced the church of Kenfig. In many churches, such as St John's in Cardiff, the remodelling was thorough enough to leave only the odd pier or doorway from previous work. The panelling sometimes found on wall surfaces and the vertical emphasis of window tracery of the period 1360 to 1540 have led to the style then in vogue being called Perpendicular.

Redwick Church

St Andrews Major

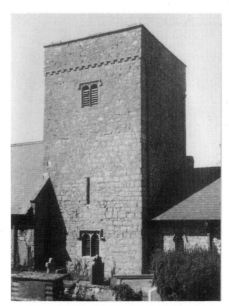

Llysworney

St Hilary

Newcastle Bridgend

Towers in the Vale of Glamorgan

Penmark Church

The period 1470 to 1540 was another boom time for building work in Welsh churches although almost all of the work consisted of remodelling, rebuilding, or adding to older structures. About half of the medieval church towers in Gwent and Glamorgan are of this period. They include fine structures at Cardiff and the marshland churches of Peterstone and St Brides Wentloog. All these have the blank panelled parapets and corner pinnacles common on church towers in adjacent parts of England but rare in Wales. Other notable work includes the Llanquian aisle at Cowbridge, the huge towers at St Brides Major and Llantrythyd, and aisles at Magor, Penalt, and Mathern, which also has a good (but not large) tower.

By 1540 most of the originally bare and poorly lighted 12th and 13th century church interiors had been transformed. The large new windows admitted more light, although some of them were filled with stained glass (now rarely surviving except in fragments) depicting biblical scenes, lives of saints or heraldic shields of benefactors. Most floors were now paved but others were still of rammed earth covered with rushes. There were now usually benches for seating the congregation, a pulpit to allow the more recently fashionable preaching of sermons, screens closing off chapels with secondary altars, and other furnishings such as chests in which plate could be locked away. The larger churches had sets of choir stalls, sometimes with hinged seats known as miserichords. Much of the woodwork and stonework was painted and combined with murals and painted coved ceilings with gilded bosses to produce a riot of colour. Most of this painting now only survives in a faded, fragmentary state and quite a lot must remain hidden under the coats of plain whitewash considered more suitable after the Reformation of the 1540s. Medieval pulpits rarely survive but there are fine screens dividing off the chancels at Bettws Newydd, Kemys Commander, Llangwm Uchaf, Redwick, Trostrey and Usk, all in Gwent. Most of them originally supported roodlofts so called from the image of the Crucifixion (or Rood) fixed upon them. These lofts were used as a stage for religious plays and as musicians' galleries, organs then being unknown in small village churches. Plays were of importance in the conveyance of God's Word to the congregation in an age when few could read, long sermons were not yet fashionable and services were mostly in Latin rather than in English or Welsh.

Little work was carried out upon the fabric of parish churches in Wales during the period 1550 to 1800 apart from minor (and often inadequate) maintenance, the insertion of a window here and there, and the occasional addition or rebuilding of a tower, porch or side chapel. Chepstow has quite an interesting early 18th century tower and several churches have late 16th or 17th century chapels containing the monuments of the lords of the manor. The round arch reappeared in the 16th century and the cusping of window lights normal in the 14th and 15th centuries gradually went out of fashion. Large round-headed windows became normal in the late 17th and 18th centuries (although examples of them are rare in South Wales), and the pointed arch along with the Gothic style in general was only reintroduced in the middle of the 19th century. There was then another building boom, with many new churches (not described in this book) being erected to serve the new industrial suburbs, whilst most of the medieval churches were drastically restored or rebuilt, and many of the furnishings that had managed to survive being cast out at the Reformation were replaced and a number of monuments either moved around, damaged, or simply thrown out. However, carved fragments from old screens and lofts sometimes found their way into new stalls, galleries, benches, chests, altar rails or a pulpit or reredos. Pulpits of c1620-40, sometimes dated, are fairly common. Some bear classical motifs, and some have a tester or sounding board above. Three decker pulpits with lower stalls for lay readers later came into fashion. Few survive but 17th and 18th century woodwork generally is fairly common, and includes altar rails, the communion tables which replaced old altar slabs, stalls, pews, galleries and panelling. Amongst fonts, Norman tubs form the largest group by far. There are quite a number of late medieval fonts, usually of octagonal form, and then there is another group of the 1660s.

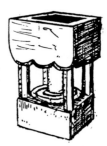

Font at Redwick

HERE LYETH THE BODIES OF WILLM PRICHARD OF LANOVOR ESQVIRE·&COF MATHEW PRICHARD OF LANOVOR ESQ. HIS SONNE AND HEIRE LINEALLY DESCENDED FROM THE BODYE OF CRADOCKE VRAICHVRAS EARLE OF HEREFORD & PRINCE BETWEENE WYE AND SEAVERNE

Brass at Llanover

Font at Bonvilston

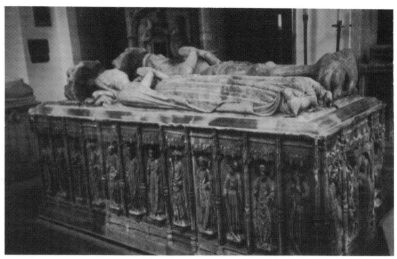

Tomb in Abergavenny Priory Church

The commonest type of medieval monument in Wales is the coffin lid with a floriated cross either incised or in relief upon it, sometimes with an inscription and other motifs such as a sword for a warrior or a chalice for a priest. Examples exist in South Wales from the 13th century to the 17th century. Early grave-slabs and cross fragments were sometimes used as sills and lintels for late medieval and post-Reformation period windows. Fully three dimensional effigies set either in a niche or upon a tomb chest are less common. The two early 13th century knights at Ewenny are the earliest of the thirty effigies that survive. Some are too damaged for accurate dating and few have remained in their original positions. Llantwit Major, St Hilary, St Athan, and Llanfihangel Rogiet each have two or three monuments but by far the best collection is in the priory church at Abergavenny. There is a fine tomb and effigy at St Brides Major, and there are 15th century brasses at Llandough and Swansea.

Fully three-dimensional effigies of the post-Reformation period are less common and tomb-chests sometimes occur without effigies. There are three tomb-chests at Margam, three damaged effigies at Raglan, and others at Abergavenny. Figures in shallow relief (sometimes crudely executed) on slabs are quite common, as at Llanvetherine and Skenfrith, and there are brass plates with figures at Llangattock and Llanover. These are poor in quality compared with the medieval cut-out figures, which are more deeply engraved. Goldcliffe has a brass plate recording a local flood and plain brass inscriptions occur here and there. A 16th century development was the wall-monument showing the deceased (or more usually a couple) kneeling in prayer. A 17th century example can be seen at Cowbridge. After the Civil Wars of the 1640s effigies of any kind were unusual and tablets became the norm. However these can be quite elaborate, with not only inscriptions but heraldry, putti, symbols of a trade or status or death or a claim to fame.

Pulpit at Pennard

GAZETTEER OF GWENT CHURCHES

ABERGAVENNY *St John* SO 300142

In the middle of the town stands the embattled tower (rebuilt c1750) of the former parish church of St John. In the 1540s St John's became the chapel of Henry VIII's new grammar school. Part of the unaisled nave also survives.

ABERGAVENNY *St Mary* SO 301141

This large cruciform church served a Benedictine priory founded by Hamelin de Ballon in the 1090s. When dissolved in 1536 the priory only had a prior and four monks. The nave was already used by the townsfolk, who then took over the whole of the church. For a while the chancel was used as a school but later became part of the church again. It and the crossing and transepts (with two bay chapels in the angle between them) are essentially 14th century work, altered after being ravaged by Owain Glyndwr in 1402, and several times restored, the east window being of 1922, the north transept window of 1954, and others are of 1896. The plain embattled central tower retains original belfry windows. The nave and north aisle retain some medieval work but the arcade of five bays and the west front and porch are of 1881-2 by Thomas Nicholson, when galleries inserted in 1828-9 were swept away.

The furnishings include a Norman font with a rope moulding and a series of radiating arcs, a huge wooden 15th century figure of Jesse, probably from a reredos, Royal Arms of Queen Anne dated 1709, and a fine set of canopied stalls made in the early 16th century for Prior Winchester, whose name appears on one of them. Earlier misericord seats were reused to make up the set.

William Baker's tomb, Abergavenny Priory

Tower of St John's Church, Abergavenny

The church contains more old effigies than any other in Wales. In the north chapel are effigies of Eva de Braose, d1257, and of a 14th century member of the Hastings family. The latter originally held an animal, said to be a squirrel. There is also an effigy of Dr David Lewis, d1584. Now moved from this chapel into the north transept is a fine wooden effigy of John, 2nd Lord Hastings, d1325. The seven main monuments in the Herbert Chapel on the south side were restored in 1994-8 and three of them were moved. There are effigies of Sir Lawrence de Hastings, d1348, and Sir William de Hastings, d1348, Sir William ap Thomas, (builder of Raglan Castle) d1446, and his wife Gwladys, d1454, Sir Richard Herbert of Coldbrook, beheaded 1469, and his wife Margaret, Richard Herbert of Ewyas, d1510, Judge Andrew Powell, d1631, and his wife, and William Baker, d1648, and his wife. The chapel floor is almost entirely paved with medieval and later gravestones.

BASSALEG   *St Basil*   ST 277872

Robert de la Haye founded a Benedictine priory here c1110, but it was abandoned in 1235 and nothing so early survives, although the arcade to the south aisle built in 1878 replaced one with "square piers and low arches", which sounds like 12th or 13th century work. The chancel has a 15th century east window with panel tracery and a 16th century south window, and there is a substantial west tower of c1500 with a segmental-headed west doorway and battlements. The organ chamber on the south side dates from a restoration of 1902-3, and the early 19th century mausoleum of the Morgans of Tredegar on the north side of the chancel was enlarged into a chapel in 1916. Eleven hatchments of members of this family are displayed in the nave and there are several fine early to mid 19th century monuments in their chapel.

Abergavenny Priory Church

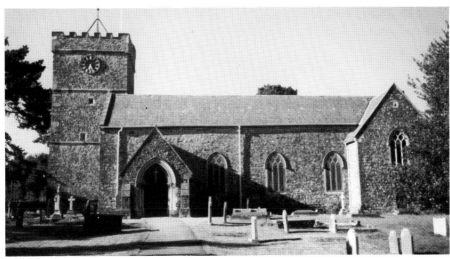

Bassaleg Church

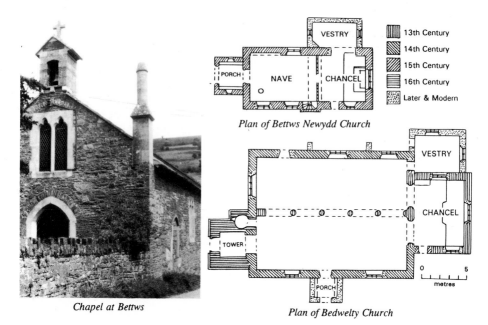

▦	13th Century
▧	14th Century
▨	15th Century
▤	16th Century
▥	Later & Modern

Plan of Bettws Newydd Church

Chapel at Bettws

Plan of Bedwelty Church

BEDWELTY   *St Sannan*   SO 166004

This hilltop church has an unusual plan, being double naved, with an embattled 16th century tower set west of the south nave, which has a porch, but with a wide chancel straddling half the width of each nave. Both naves have restored 14th century windows, and there must have been an earlier tower, since the tower arch is of that date. The crude five bay arcade dividing them is 13th century, and with it go the arches from each nave into the chancel. Probably the original 13th century layout had two further arches to create a narrow chancel and chapel, and the then nave and aisle were narrower than the present naves. The north vestry was added in 1909. There is a chest of c1500 with symbols of the Passion in the chancel.

BERTHOLEY   *St Bartholomew*   ST 393948

This chapel-of-ease to Llantrisant became a cowshed in the 18th century but collapsed in the early 20th century. In a field a minimal remains of a small nave with a chancel the same width internally but with thinner walls.

BETTWS   *Dedication Unknown*   SO 297193

This chapel-of-ease to Llantilio Pertholey was mostly rebuilt in 1829. The south doorway with a four-centred head was blocked in 1893, when a triple east lancet was created from 13th century parts with a keeled roll-moulding.

BETTWS   *St David*   ST 289904

This small church was a chapel-of-ease to Newport until the 17th century. Probably 13th century, although the nave and chancel are of different builds, it has 19th century windows and a west porch and south vestry of 1974.

Chapel at Bettws

BETTWS NEWYDD   *Dedication Unknown*   SO 362058

There is a Norman font with circles and a rope moulding set on a 15th century base. The walls may be partly Norman since the west wall has slight traces of a older roof than the present wagon roof, and in 1952 foundations were revealed of an early east wall beyond the present one. Otherwise this is a single chamber 15th century building with a west porch and a fine east window, although by far its most notable feature is the complete survival of both screen and loft reached by steps on the south side. The loft front is decorated with foliage bands of vine and oak and pierced vertical panels of tracery. The rood or crucifix on the loft was removed in the 1540s.

BISHTON   *St Cadwalladr*   ST 387873

The nave has trefoil-headed lancets of 1300. The tower may be of c1400 since its belfry windows are Decorated in style, whilst the west doorway is fully-fledged Perpendicular. The north porch, two south windows in the nave, the east window and the tower west window are 19th century. The font is late medieval.

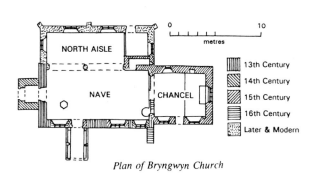

NORTH AISLE

NAVE   CHANCEL

0   10

metres

13th Century
14th Century
15th Century
16th Century
Later & Modern

Plan of Bryngwyn Church

Arcade in Bedwelty Church

BRYNGWYN   *St Peter*   SO 390094

According to Geraldus Cambrensis churches were founded in the mid 12th century by Aeddan Gweathfoed, Lord of Clytha, at Bettws Newydd, Bryngwyn and Clytha. At Bryngwyn the earliest features now remaining are the 13th century west doorway and surmounting lancet now looking into a tiny 14th century embattled tower. The chancel is 15th century, with a three-light east window, and so are the south doorway and porch and one south window. The north aisle with its two bay arcade and the vestry east of it (flanking the old roodloft staircase) is of 1871 by John Pritchard, and the chancel arch is of 1854. The hexagonal font with shields and a panelled base and stem is late medieval and there are late 17th century altar rails. In the vestry are tablets to Frances Frampton, d1665, and Thomas Jenkins, d1779. There is also a stone to William Tyler, d1695, and there is an old iron-bound chest.

BUCKHOLT   *St John*   ST 510154

The small simple church of 1889 contains an octagonal font dated 1663 with rosettes and names of churchwardens. It is said to have come from Dixton.

CAERLEON   *St Cadoc*   ST 339906

The oldest parts of this large church lying in the middle of the former Roman fortress of Isca are the 13th century tower in the west bay of the south aisle, against which one and a half unmoulded arches of the Norman south arcade survive, with one rectangular pier. The tower has three levels of lancets. The arcades were otherwise rebuilt in the 15th century, when the tower was given its embattled top stage and the aisles were widened. A rebuilding in 1867-8 by Seddon has swept away the old furnishings and left only a little medieval masonry in the west and north walls, plus parts of arcades (of four full bays on the north side) with four shafts on the piers and wave-mouldings on the arches. Seddon also added the south porch. The chancel, which had already been rebuilt in the 1850s, was extended in 1932-5 and given a chapel on the south and spacious vestries on the north.

CAERWENT   *St Stephen and St Tathan*   ST 468905

The disc crosshead discovered SE of the church and now in the south aisle may be a relic of the monastery recorded here in the 10th century. The oldest parts of the church are the east wall with two lancets of the much altered chancel and the three bay south arcade of the nave. The chancel once had chapels on either side, and there are blocked late medieval arches on the south side, against which now abut vestries of 1910-12, when the south aisle was also rebuilt. The chancel north wall with its row of lancets is of the 1840s. Of the 15th century is the nave north wall, with a pointed headed window and a square-headed window (both of three lights) set either side of a diagonally buttressed porch with a stair in the east wall to a gallery which gave access to a statue niche over the inner doorway. The ogival-headed stoup beside the inner doorway is a reset 14th century piece. The embattled west tower with corner gargoyles and a polygonal SE stair-turret is of later in the 15th century. The pulpit dated 1632 has initials of churchwardens and a series of cartouches. The font bowl is probably Norman, recut in the 18th century, and set on a late medieval base. In the porch is the base of a former statue of c220 showing Tiberius Claudius Paulinus, who commanded the Second Augustan Legion (based at Caerleon), and there is a small section of Roman mosaic in the south aisle, where there is also the head of a 15th century churchyard cross.

Bryngwyn Church

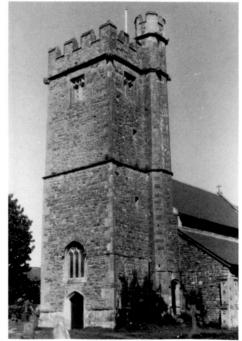

Caerleon Church

Caerwent Church

Chepstow Priory Church

Caldicot Church

CALDICOT   *St Mary*   ST 484886

The Norman central tower retains one original round-headed window on the south side. The chancel is 14th century, although the south windows of that date are renewed, and the northern ones blocked up. The nave was also rebuilt in the 14th century, the west window having cusped ogival reticulated tracery, whilst one south window is early Perpendicular in style. The tower arches are also 14th century. In the 15th century the tower was heightened, a new east window provided, a large porch added on the south side of the nave, along with new windows either side of it, and a north aisle added. The five bay arcade with lozenge-shaped piers with embattled capitals on the shafts remains, but the aisle was rebuilt in 1857-8 by Henry Woodyer, who added the pyramidal cap to the tower. A vestry added north of the tower in 1911 was extended beside the chancel in 1928. Set in the porch SE corner is a damaged effigy of a medieval priest.

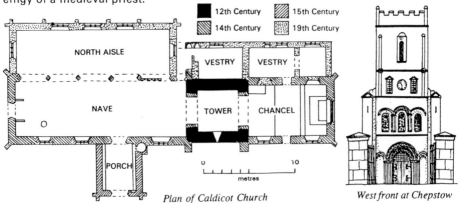

Plan of Caldicot Church

West front at Chepstow

CHEPSTOW   *St Mary*   ST 536940

Of the church of a Benedictine priory founded either by William Fitz-Osbern or his son Roger de Breteuil before 1075 there remain five bays of an aisled Norman nave with huge rectangular piers carrying plain arcade arches of two orders. There is a triforium, more complex on the south than on the north, and then a clerestory. The piers show evidence of cut-away imposts which once carried a vault over the nave. The choir was demolished after the priory was suppressed in 1536, but the central tower survived until it fell in 1701 and destroyed the transepts. In 1705-6 the nave east end was closed off and a new tower built up within and over the westernmost bay. The tower west wall consequently has a Norman doorway of several orders with chevrons flanked by blind arches at ground level, three Norman windows above, and then a pair of 18th century windows with gabled heads flanking a clock. The tower arch facing east also incorporates a lot of reused Norman material. The aisles (also rib-vaulted) were demolished during a remodelling of 1838-41, which added new transepts, a short chancel, and filled the nave with galleries. The latter were removed in another campaign begun in 1890 when a new chancel was built between the vestries added in 1880, and the south transept was remodelled. Just one bay of the south aisle had been reinstated by 1913, when the work was abandoned. The transepts are divided off by two bay arcades and the northern arcade pier stands on the massive base of the original NW pier of the former central tower.

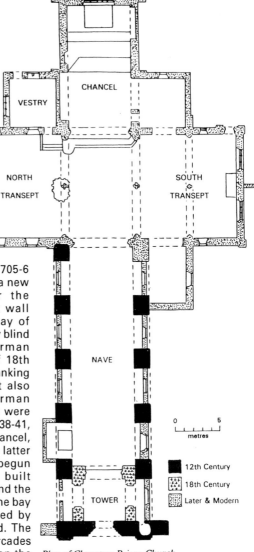

Plan of Chepstow Priory Church

There are two fonts, one 12th century and the other 15th century. There are recumbent effigies of the 2nd Earl of Worcester, d1549, and his wife, and of Margaret Cleyton, d1627, although her two husbands are depicted kneeling. This monument was made before she died, being dated 1620. The many other monuments include those of Francis Davis, 1766, Susanna Higfoot, 1779, Sophia Price, d1787, and (in the tower ringing chamber) Mary Harvey, 1712, and Richard Vaughan, d1713.

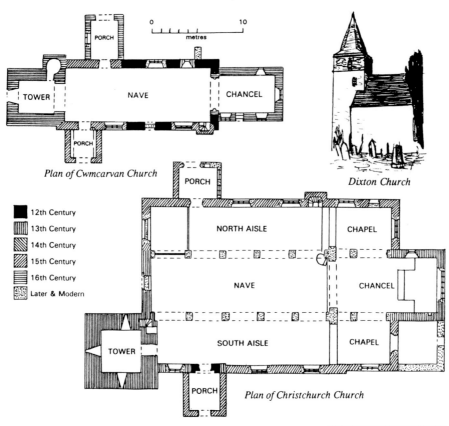

0   10
metres

Plan of Cwmcarvan Church

Dixton Church

■ 12th Century
▥ 13th Century
▨ 14th Century
▧ 15th Century
▤ 16th Century
▦ Later & Modern

Plan of Christchurch Church

CHRISTCHURCH   *Holy Trinity*   ST 347894

This is one of the largest medieval churches in Gwent but has seen much rebuilding and renewal of arcades, windows and roofs as a result of fires in 1877 and 1949, the latter an arson attack. The chancel has a 13th century piscina, one original north lancet, and the bases remain of three in the east wall. The south aisle must also have existed by then since the lower part of the huge tower at the west end of it has blocked 13th century lancets. Reset in the aisle is a nook-shafted Norman doorway with chevrons on the main arch. The north aisle may also be of 13th century origin but the outer wall is 15th century, with a roodloft staircase, and the tower top and the two porches are also of that date, although the north porch has been much altered. In the south chapel is a worn incised slab depicting John and Isabella Colmer, d1376. This stone was thought to have powers of healing on the Eve of Ascension Day and as late as 1770 sixteen ill children were laid upon it in the hope of a cure.

Incised slab at Christchurch

Cwmcarvan Church

Christchurch Church

CLYTHA   *St Aeddan*   SO 368094

Not far north of Clytha Park are a few piles of stone in a field, all that remains of a single chamber. Cut stones from the windows and doorways found on the site suggest a later medieval date.

CRICK   *St Nyven*   ST 490903

A small 13th century manorial single chamber chapel with two east lancets was adapted into a barn in the 18th century and has now been converted into a house.

CWMCARVAN   *St Catwg*   SO 477075

The blocked doorway on the south side suggests that the nave is Norman and has been lengthened westwards in the 15th century. Of that later period are the two porches (not in line with each other, and one now a vestry), the roodloft staircase, the octagonal font, the ribbed wagon roof, and two square-headed three-light windows with hoodmoulds on the south side. The ashlar-faced west tower of three stages with a NE stair turret rising above the battlements with a decorative moulding is early 16th century, although the tower arch is probably early 14th century and contains a screen made up of Jacobean arcaded panels. The chancel features seem to be of that period also, although this part was rebuilt in 1872. The nave north wall has one late 13th century lancet and a larger window of 1879.

Cwmyoy Church

Plaster panel at Cwmyoy

CWMYOY   *St Martin*   SO 299233

The church lies on a south-facing slope above the Honddu so affected by landslips that the walls now lean at a variety of crazy angles. Even with the support of huge flying buttresses it is difficult to imagine how the 13th century west tower has remained standing. The south doorway with a roll-moulded segmental head, one small north window and the egg-shaped font are all Norman. One south window is of c1300, and the impressive nave roof and the roughly-made south porch may be of the same period. Another window, of three lights under a square hoodmould, is 16th century. Four steps lead up into the chancel, which is 13th century with one plain south lancet and a cusped northern one, whilst the east window with two ogival-headed lights is 14th century. Of the 17th century are the plaster panels in the porch and the altar rails in the chancel, where there are tablets to Thomas Price, dated 1682, William Griffiths, d1774, James Prosser, d1775, and several others.

DINGESTOW   *St Dingat*   SO 457104

The west tower was added in 1846 and the north transept in 1887-8, and the rest appears to be all restored or rebuilt apart from one three-light window on the south and a narrower loop beside it which lighted the rood loft.

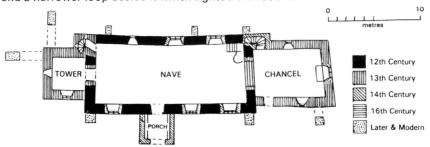

0   10
metres

TOWER   NAVE   CHANCEL

PORCH

■ 12th Century
▓ 13th Century
▨ 14th Century
▤ 16th Century
▦ Later & Modern

Plan of Cwmyoy Church

Cwmyoy Church

DIXTON   *St Peter*   SO 520136

The church lies by the Wye, shielded from the busy A40 by trees, and is first referred to as early as the 8th century. The herringbone masonry in the nave north wall is probably 11th century. The rendered nave was probably lengthened when the small west tower with one lancet and a broach-spire was built in the late 13th century. The chancel has a late 14th century window on each side. The north porch and adjacent vestry are of 1824, and the south porch and two windows east of it are of 1861-21, but the window west of it is 14th century. There are old wagon roofs. The Royal Arms are dated 1711 and there is a relief of St Peter's martyrdom in the north porch.

GOETRE   *St Peter*   SO 327059

Only a Norman font with circles above a rope-moulding and an old chest survived the rebuilding of 1845-6. The church lies in a grove of yew trees.

GOLDCLIFF   *St Mary Magdalene*   ST 365832

In the chancel is a brass plate recording that "On the 20th day of January, 1606, even as it came to pass, it pleased God the flud (tide) did flow to the edge of this same brass, and in this parish there was lost £5000 in stock etc, besides 22 people drowned". The church itself was built anew shortly after an earlier flood in 1424 had partly destroyed a priory founded in 1113 by Robert de Chandos. From the priory must have come the two pieces of 12th century fretwork inserted in the south wall c1850. The ceiling is 18th century, and perhaps also the west tower. The windows (c1880, when the single body was divided into a nave and chancel by inserting arch. The medieval font has an 18th century cover.

Grosmont Church

GROSMONT   *St Nicholas*   SO 405243

This is a large cruciform church with an aisled nave five bays long, built in the 13th century for a place that long aspired to be a town, but has remained only a village. The nave and aisles, which have arcades of double-chamfered arches on circular piers, remain roofed but lie empty, the eastern parts providing enough space for modern services. In the early 1870s the chancel was rebuilt by J.P.Seddon using old parts including a double piscina and sets of four and three lancets in the north wall, the large south chapel was totally rebuilt as a vestry, and the tower arches and piers mostly rebuilt to save the octagonal 14th century superstructure and spire from collapse. A second campaign in 1878 saw the partial rebuilding of the transepts, which have unusual western aisles, and the repair of the nave. The three-light end window in the north transept, however, is original work of c1300, and there is a fine 13th century north doorway with a 14th century porch in front of it. The west front is original too, with a central doorway, pilasters where the arcades adjoin, lancets to the aisles, and a 14th century window with reticulated tracery over the doorway. In the south transept is an unfinished effigy of a late 13th or early 14th century knight and there is also a slab to Charles William and his wife Joan dated 1636 (and also 1708). There are many old ledger stones in the nave on one of the Victorian south windows in the south aisle has a grave slab as its sill. Upon it sits a late medieval carved Virgin and Child. The font may be Norman, but seems to have been altered.

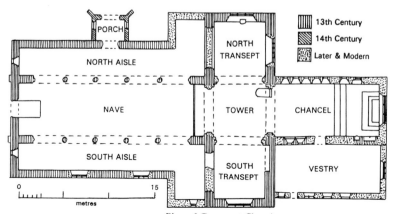

Plan of Grosmont Church

GWERNESNEY *St Michael* SO 415017

The nave and chancel are both of c1300, the west and south doorways and the windows with trefoiled heads to the lights on the east and north all being of that period. Two heads on the west doorway could be older work reset. Two south windows, the nave roof, and the porch are 15th century. The screen and one window west of the porch are 16th century, whilst the chancel roof could be 17th century. The double bellcote is of 1853. The font has an old base and is enclosed by medieval screens and there are 17th century altar rails.

HENLLYS *St Peter* ST 267911

The church lies far south of the village with just one farm beside it. It consists of a nave and chancel, both 13th century but perhaps of different builds, and a 15th century west tower with NE stair turret rising higher and a blocked west doorway. The tower west window and the chancel east window are similar in design. The chancel has traces of old wall-paintings. The south porch is probably 16th century and the window west of it may be 17th century.

ITTON *St Deiniol* ST 494953

The tower arch and the chancel are 14th century, and the tower itself has a west window with Y-tracery and a polygonal NE stair-turret. The south porch is of c1500. The windows are mostly of Henry Woodyer's restoration of 1869, when a vestry was added and arches provided on either side of the chancel arch. The oldest of the monuments to the Curres is to John, d1726, i.e before they purchased Itton Court.

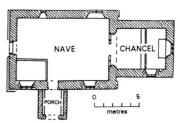

Plan of Gwernesney Church

Henllys Church

KEMYS COMMANDER   *All Saints*   SO 349048

The hexagonal font could be 14th century but the tiny single chamber church (originally dedicated to St John the Baptist) seems to be entirely late 15th century. Original are the three-light east window, other windows of two and three lights with square heads and a blocked priest's doorway on the south, the west doorway and timber-framed porch, the wagon roof and the screen.

KEMYS INFERIOR   *All Saints*   ST 381928

Hidden in woods between the A449 and the River Wye are foundations of a church demolished in 1960-2. Mullioned windows with arched lights were transferred to Kemys Manor, and a three-light 15th century window was reset in the garden wall.

KILGWRRWG   *Holy Cross*   ST 463985

The internally battered walls and the shape of the blocked west doorway suggest a 13th century date for the small nave and chancel, which are divided just by a solid roof truss. The south doorway and one three-light window on each side are 15th century. The porch is said to be of 1871, although it has a medieval outer arch.

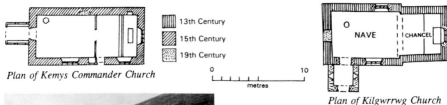

13th Century
15th Century
19th Century

Plan of Kemys Commander Church

0   metres   10

Plan of Kilgwrrwg Church

NAVE   CHANCEL

Llanarth Church

Kilgwrrwg Church

LANGSTONE   *Dedication Unknown*   ST 372892

The nave and chancel are 14th century, with one reset trefoil-headed north window. Several two-light windows and the south porch are 15th century. The nave was extended westwards in 1622, the date that appears on the timber west doorway, probably to accommodate a gallery. The north chapel and vestry are 19th century, and the octagonal font is 18th century. At Cats Ash (ST 372907) is a chapel of St Curig with a blocked 14th century east window, now part of a house of 1604.

LLANARTH   *St Teilo*   SO 375109

The large nave and comparatively small chancel are 14th century, both having foiled lancets and original south doorways. The south porch is also 14th century. The nave has two 15th century windows on the south side and three of 1847 (but with medieval rere-arches) on the north. The hexagonal font has panelling on the stem and base. The ashlar-faced west tower with a NE stair turret is 16th century, although the battlements and pinnacles are of 1884-5. There is also an old chest.

LLANBADOC   *St Madoc*   SO 376001

The church lies below a lane beside the Usk south of the town of Usk. The nave has a 14th century west doorway and trefoiled lancet above, both now looking into a slender tower with corbelled battlements which may be as late as the 16th century. The porch outer arch may also be 14th century. Both nave and chancel have square-headed south windows of the 15th century. The east window was modified in 1872 by John Pritchard, who added a north aisle of three bays and a north vestry. The font and the outermost recesses of the reredos are also medieval.

Llanbadoc Church

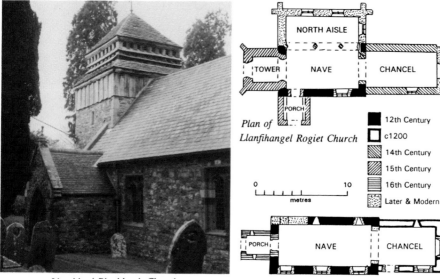

Plan of Llanfihangel Rogiet Church

12th Century
c1200
14th Century
15th Century
16th Century
Later & Modern

0   10
metres

Llanddewi Rhydderch Church

Plan of Llandegfedd Church

LLANDDEWI FACH   *St David*   SO 332958

This small disused nave-and-chancel church was mostly rebuilt by J.P.Seddon in 1856-7 and only the round-headed 16th century west doorway is untampered with, although the square-headed windows represent what was there before.

LLANDDEWI RHYDDERCH   *St David*   SO 349129

The Norman west tower has tiny original windows on either side, a 14th century tower arch, and a later recessed timber framed top with a pyramidal roof. The nave and chancel are a 14th century rebuilding, probably wider than the Norman originals. The east wall has triple cusped lancets but the south doorways, porch and windows are 15th century, whilst the north side was rebuilt in 1862-3 by J.P.Seddon. The font has foliated spurs on its base. The earliest of several rather rustic tablets is that of Seth Powell, d1785. The base and part of the shaft remain of a churchyard cross.

LLANDDEWI SKIRRID   *St David*   SO 341170

The rebuilding of 1879 by John Pritchard has left only a medieval west tower and a Norman font bowl decorated with chevrons and set on a 15th century base and stem. Very slight traces of a chapel of St Michael lie on the summit of Skirrid Fawr.

LLANDEGFEDD   *St Tegfeth*   SO 339958

The church was mostly rebuilt in 1875 by E.A.Lansdowne, but the nave has a Norman north window, and the chancel another of c1200, and there are 16th century windows in the south and east walls, a will of 1541 having left money for glazing the chancel windows. The priest's doorway, and the west doorway and porch are also 16th century. The plain pulpit is 18th century and there are some old box-pews. Amongst several 18th century tablets is that to David Williams, d1729.

LLANDENNY   *St John*   SO 415039

The position of the Norman south doorway with a solid semicircular tympanum suggests that the nave was lengthened westwards in the 15th century, the period of the porch and two south windows. There is also one tiny Norman north window. The chancel of c1300 has single and paired lancets with trefoiled heads. The embattled west tower with a NE stair-turret is 16th century. The font dated 1661 has cartouches on the sides of the octagonal bowl and floral patterns incised on the stem. The north vestry is of 1860. There is a cartouche to Roger Otes, d1706 and his son, d1710, and an 18th century tablet to David Lewis and his family.

LLANDERFEL   *St Derfel*   ST 264953

Slight traces of an L-shaped building lie west of a farm beside a track from Upper Cwmbran to Henllys. Derfel Gadarn, a veteran of King Arthur's battles against Mordred, is said to have retired here.

LLANELLEN   *St Helen*   SO 304109

The nave windows, the wagon roof, the roodloft staircase and the south doorway and porch are all 15th century. In 1850-1 John Pritchard rebuilt the chancel and added a vestry and a new west bay to the nave with a spired turret on top of it. An old font has been adapted to serve as a sundial.

LLANELLI   *St Elli*   ST 233148

This church lay in Breconshire until 1974. The south walls of the small nave and chancel are probably 13th century, whilst the north aisle and chapel have a continuous late medieval wagon roof and two unrestored 15th century windows. The 16th century west tower is wider than the nave and a SW stair turret with a timber-framed gablet projects still further south. The tower has a slated spire of 1897. The font is probably Norman and there is a fine Jacobean altar table. In the sanctuary are two slabs of the 1630s and 40s with figures in shallow relief, and there is also a wall monument to Edward Lewis, d1713.

LLANFAIR DISCOED   *St Mary*   ST 447924

The medieval church was mostly rebuilt in 1746, and after a another rebuilding in 1882-3 only the south doorway and the jambs of the porch outer entrance remain of it. The hexagonal font is probably 18th century. The oldest monument is of c1808.

LLANFAIR KILGEDDIN   *St Mary*   SO 356087

The church lies in a wide bend of the River Usk far from the village it served. It is no longer in regular use, but has been restored and preserved as a monument mainly because of Heywood Sumner's fine wall decorations of 1888-90 throughout the whole building using a sgraffito technique to illustrate the Benedicte. On the south side the features are mostly the work of J.D.Sedding in 1873-6 (as are most of the furnishings), but he reused old jambs in the doorway of his extension to the nave, two 15th century windows remain in the nave north wall, and the chancel has a late 13th century north window with plate tracery and a mostly late medieval roof. The hexagonal font with shields on the panelled base and its cover are late medieval, and there is a much restored 14th century screen brought in from elsewhere.

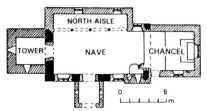

Llanfihangel Rogiet Church

Plan of Llanfihangel Gobion Church

Llanfihangel Gobion Church

LLANFIHANGEL CRUCORNEY   *St Michael*   SO 325206

Since a crosswall was built in 1976 the western three bays of the long nave have been left roofless. The paired lancets are of the rebuilding of 1835 but an original 13th century doorway and lancet above look into the tall 15th century west tower. The tower battlements lie on a string course with gargoyles in the form of human heads at the corners. The porch is also 15th century. Despite rebuilding in 1884-6 the chancel has a 13th century single lancet on each side and a cusped pair on the north. A worn slab of c1600 has reliefs of a man and woman praying towards a cross, and there is a wall monument to Richard Scudamore, d1695.

Llanfihangel Gobion Church

LLANFIHANGEL GOBION   *St Michael*   347092

The NE and SW corners of the nave are probably Norman. The south doorway looks 14th century. Of the 15th century are the pyramidal-roofed west tower, the font, the roodloft stair, the roofs, most of the windows, and the narrow north aisle with an arcade of timber posts to carry the nave north wall-plate. One north window has carvings of a heart and shears in the spandrels and another has intertwined hearts, whilst at the SW corner is a carving showing angels guiding a soul up to heaven.

LLANFIHANGEL PONTYMOEL   *St Michael*   SO 465018

The internally battered nave south wall may be 12th or 13th century. The double bellcote is carried on a thick west wall pierced by a doorway flanked by two blind arches internally. There are plastered ribbed wagon roofs of medieval type, although there is said to have been a rebuilding in 1736 (the year that appears over the south porch outer entrance), and there was a restoration in 1904, when a vestry was added. The nailhead on the font may be a 13th century recutting of a Norman bowl.

LLANFIHANGEL ROGIET   *St Michael*   ST 452878

The disused church is surrounded by farm buildings. The chancel has one 14th century window but the east wall has been rebuilt. Also 14th century are two arches of the arcade, east of which is a third narrower arch of c1500 probably built in connection with a screen and loft. The aisle itself was rebuilt in 1904. The font, the embattled and diagonally buttressed west tower and the round-arched south doorway are also probably of c1500, although the porch may be older. There is a 15th century tomb with a 14th century effigy of Anne Martel, d1270, whilst the damaged effigy of a crosslegged knight may be her husband John.

Llanfihangel Pontymoel Church

LLANFIHANGEL-TOR-Y-MYNYDD   *St Michael*   SO 465018

The nave, chancel and south porch are all 15th century, the best feature being the moulded outer arch of the porch. One three-light mullioned window is 16th century. The 17th century altar rails survived the restoration of 1853. The last remains of another church by the farm at Llangunnog, 1km SW, had vanished by 1939.

LLANFIHANGEL-YSTERN-LLEWERN   *St Michael*   SO 433138

Although rebuilt in 1874 the chancel retains a 14th century east window with cusped Y-tracery. The nave south doorway could also be 14th century. The square-headed window of three cinquefoiled lights east of it is early 16th century, and the wagon roof on moulded wall-plates but with tie-beams as well could also be of that date. One beam at the west end supports a timber-framed belfry. The chancel has an old piscina and there are a stoup and old font in the nave. On the north wall is a rustic relief to rector William Hopkins, d1698, with three pistols on the coat of arms above.

LLANFOIST   *St Helen*   SO 287132

The south doorway, one north window and the roodloft stair are 15th century and one south window is 16th century. A vestry was added during the 1872 restoration. In the churchyard is an unusually complete medieval cross, lacking just the head.

LLANFRECHFA   *All Saints*   ST 321936

A rebuilding and enlargement of 1873-4, when the church was lengthened, and given a north aisle and huge north vestry, have left only the 15th century west tower with a NE stair turret, and the doorway and porch at the SW corner, which are probably 14th century. The furnishings and monuments are all 19th century.

Llangattock Lingoed Church

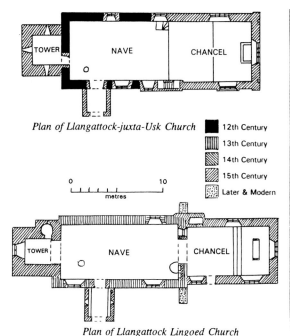

Plan of Llangattock-juxta-Usk Church

■ 12th Century

▨ 13th Century

▨ 14th Century

▨ 15th Century

▨ Later & Modern

0   10
metres

Plan of Llangattock Lingoed Church

Llangattock-juxta-Usk Church

LLANGATTOCK LINGOED   *St Cadoc*   SO 362200

The chancel arch is 13th or 14th century and belong to a chancel narrower than the present one with fine 15th century three light windows containing fragments of old stained glass to the east and south. There is a squint north of the chancel arch, whilst south of it is a recess and piscina for a nave altar. The nave features, including the wagon roof and south doorway and porch are also 15th century, as is the west tower with a moulded plinth, NE stair turret and battlements set on a moulded corbelled course. The bressumer carved with vine trails remains of the former rood loft. The chancel pews are dated 1634, and the tower arch (which is probably older than the tower itself) has a screen made up of various bits, including two date panels of 1593 and 1617. There are faded royal arms painted over the chancel arch. There are several 18th century tablets signed by four different makers.

LLANGATTOCK-JUXTA-USK   *St Cadoc*   SO 330097

In 1827 the nave roof was made flush with that of the chancel (they are the same width), and the top of the pyramidal-roofed tower probably also dates from then. The east window is of 1865, but the other windows and the roodloft staircase are late medieval. The chancel south window is set in a projection and there are two small openings in the outside of the east wall. The font appears to have a 13th century bowl and stem on a later medieval hexagonal base. The west wall is adorned with many tiles in eight different patterns, one being dated 1456. The monuments include a floriated cross-slab by the font, a brass plate depicting Zirophaeniza Mathewe, wife of Andrew Powell, d1625, a relief of the Reverend Herbert Jones, d1644, and a wall-monument to Robert Lucas, d1750, and his wife, d1770.

HIC IACET ZIROPHÆNIZA FILIA WILL
HELMI MATHEWE DE RADYR IN COMITA
GLAMORGAN ARMIG NVPER VXOR AN=
DREÆ POWELL ARMIG QVÆ OBIIT DECI
OCTAVO DIE MENSIS FEBRVARII ANNO
VICESSIMO SECVNDO IACOBI REGIS

Brass at Llangattock-juxta-Usk

Llangattock-Vibon-Avel Church

LLANGATTOCK-VIBON-AVEL   *St Cadoc*   SO 457157

Only a south porch-tower of c1300 (with a 16th century upper window) and a few tablets, including a brass plate to Thomas Evans, d1629, survived the rebuilding of the church in 1852-3 and the addition in 1875 of the north aisle, organ chamber, porch to the family chapel on the south side, and the chancel east end. This work was done for the Rolls family of The Hendre, behind which the church hides.

LLANGEVIEW   *St David*   SO 397007

The small nave and chancel have 15th century features and there is a west porch and a roodloft, but the blocked north doorway suggests that the nave has 12th or 13th century masonry. The 18th century furnishings include box pews (with a squire's pew in the chancel), the pulpit and reading desk, and the altar rails. One south window is Victorian. Now redundant, the church has been preserved as a monument.

LLANGOVAN   *St Govan*   SO 456055

The nave and chancel are divided by a round arch and have 13th century lancets on the north. The chancel also has two 14th century windows and one 15th century one. The ogival-headed stoup shows that the church was originally entered from the west, where there is a 15th century doorway and two piers supporting a stone belfry. The south doorway and porch reusing older materials are thought to be of c1625. There is a monument to John Ayleworth, who died in the 1680s. See page 36.

Llangovan Church

LLANGUA   *St James*   SO 390257

The church lies alone beside the Monnow near the A465. The font is Norman and the south doorway also looks Norman externally, although it could be 18th century, like the porch, and its rere-arch looks 14th century. The wider and more thinly walled chancel is probably 16th century, the period of the east window with three uncusped lights. Both nave and chancel have wagon roofs with black painted ribs and small octagonal bosses. There is a pretty 17th century timber-framed bell-turret at the west end. The Royal Arms are probably late 17th century.

Llangua Church

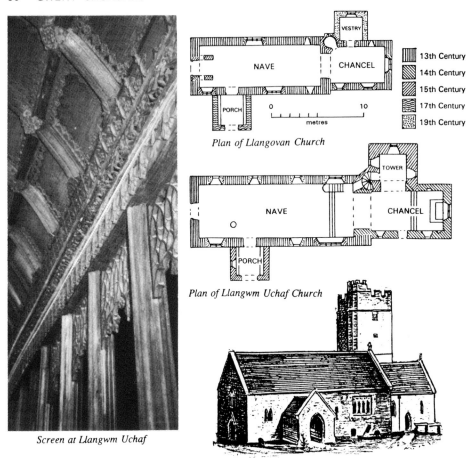

Plan of Llangovan Church

13th Century
14th Century
15th Century
17th Century
19th Century

Plan of Llangwm Uchaf Church

Screen at Llangwm Uchaf

Llangwm Uchaf Church

LLANGWM ISAF   *St John*   SO 429006

Two churches only a kilometre apart at Llangwm Isaf and Llangwm Uchaf are both
mentioned as early as 1128. The single chamber at St John's was rebuilt from a state
of ruin by John Pritchard in 1849-51 and has no old features except a west porch.

LLANGWM UCHAF   *St Jerome*   SO 434006

The nave may be 13th century in origin but it and a 15th century south porch were
mostly rebuilt in 1863-9 by Seddon apart from one large 15th century south window.
The chancel is perhaps 14th century since the chancel arch is of that date, and has a
multi-chamfered arch supported on green man corbels. The arch is mostly hidden
by a splendid late 15th century screen and rood loft much restored in 1876-8. The
loft is reached from the spiral stair in a SW turret of a contemporary embattled
tower added against the chancel north wall, through which there is a squint towards
the altar. The hourglass shaped stone with a trellis pattern found in a wall during
rebuilding may be Early Norman.

LLANGYBI *St Cybi* ST 374967

The nave may have older masonry but its features are mostly late medieval, the period of the chancel of the same width and the west tower with a SE stair-turret. There is a stoup by the inner doorway. Nearby is a blocked doorway in the south wall. The wide chancel arch was built integrally with a staircase up to the roodloft on either side, west of which are fine pointed headed windows of three lights. There are original wall paintings of Christ of the Trades in the chancel and of the Virgin weighing down St Michael's scales in favour of the blessed in the chancel, although they are partly covered by 17th century inscriptions. The font is dated 1662 and there is a pulpit of the same period with a tester, and the altar rails are of c1700. There are cartouches to Lady Elizabeth Williams, 1685, and John Francklyn, d1707, and a tablet to Sir John Williams, d1738.

LLANHENNOCK *St John* ST 354927

Except for the south doorway the nave was rebuilt in 1862-3 by Pritchard and Seddon, who added a north aisle and vestries. The chancel has an east window and blocked priest's doorway of the 15th century, and the embattled west tower with a NE stair turret is also of that period.

LLANHILLETH *St Illtyd* ST 218020

The church was closed in 1957 but has been restored for use as a hall. On the south side of the nave are traces of what was probably a 13th century doorway, and two renewed 15th century windows. Also 15th century are the chancel with an original three-light east window and a blocked loop on the south, and the wagon roofs.

Llanhennock Church

LLANISHEN   *St Denis*   SO 475032

The church and its contents are of the 1850s by Pritchard and Seddon but the base and part of the shaft remain of a medieval churchyard cross.

LLANLLOWELL   *St Llywell*   ST 393986

The small single chamber is Norman, with a tiny west window and a south doorway with geometrical patterns scratched on the lintel. The font is also of that period. The north wall was mostly rebuilt by John Pritchard in 1871-2 but contains a small 13th century lancet. The restored east window with three trefoil-headed lights is of c1300. Of the 15th century are the roodloft stair projection, the window west of it with a hoodmould on square stops, and the priest's doorway.

LLANMARTIN   *St Martin*   ST 395894

The embattled west tower with a polygonal NE stair-turret and the reset vestry doorway and parts of the chancel arch are 15th century. Seddon rebuilt the rest in 1857-8 except for a arch on the south side of the chancel which led to a chapel built under the terms of a will of 1541 of Sir William Morgan. It was ruinous by the 18th century. The arch contains fragments of a monument to his father Thomas, d1510.

LLANOVER   *St Bartholomew*   SO 318094

The ogival-headed piscinas in both nave and chancel, the south doorway with sunk quadrant mouldings and one renewed trefoil-headed lancet in the chancel all suggest an early 14th century date. The fine ashlar-faced and embattled west tower with a NE stair-turret, the east window and the wagon roofs with moulded ribs and embattled wall plates are all 15th century. The Norman font has a cable-moulding and daisies and wheels. The altar rails are dated c1700 and the south porch is dated 1750. Let into the side of one of two late 16th century oak box pews is a brass of 1600 depicting William & Matthew Pritchard in armour (see p10). Another inscription refers to Walter Ramsey, made a judge in 1631, dismissed by Parliament in 1647, but reinstated at the Restoration of Charles II in 1660, shortly before his death.

Llanover Church

LLANSANTFFRAID   *St Bridget*   SO 357009

There is a Norman font with semicircles and a rope moulding and the small nave and chancel may be Norman also. The chancel has 15th century windows and on the east wall are alabaster panels depicting the Entombment and Resurrection, probably once part of a reredos. The nave windows, chancel arch and the tiny vaulted west porch date from Pritchard and Seddon's restoration of 1856-7. The screen of 1931 contains medieval parts and there is an 18th century pulpit. There are many 17th century gravestones, including two of 1624 and 1684 to families named Jones.

LLANSOY   *St Tysoi*   SO 442023

The nave, chancel and south porch are all essentially 15th century work. There are three original doorways (including one now looking into a crudely built west tower probably no older than the 19th century), a stoup in the porch, and a roodloft staircase on the south side. The vestry and two north windows, plus several furnishings, are of 1858 by Seddon, There are 18th century altar rails.

LLANTARNAM   *St Michael*   ST 307932

The nave has one early blocked north window. The nave and chancel each have one 15th century window but two others in the nave look 16th century, and thus go with the west tower with a NE stair-turret. The east window appears to be of 1869. The north chapel is much wider than the chancel and has an arcade of depressed four-centred arches which looks 16th century, although the remains of a large blocked east window suggest a 13th century origin for the chapel. It contains fragments of a late 16th century monument and other monuments to Martin Kuyck van Meirop, d1775, and Mary Kemys, d1798. The font appears made up of medieval parts.

LLANTHONY   *St David*   SO 288279

At first sight this appears to be an unusually little altered nave and chancel church of c1180-1200 with several rounded headed windows on each side, a pair in the east wall and two doorways out of line with each other. In fact the nave originally formed the infirmary of the Augustinian abbey lying in ruins just to the north and the chancel served it as a chapel. Indeed closer inspection reveals that the window heads are post-medieval, for they originally rose into gables in the roof, and that the chancel arch is rebated for doors. The north porch is an addition of 1886-7. The font is medieval, and there are altar rails and several minor memorials of the 18th century.

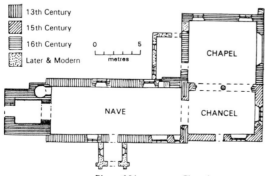

Plan of Llantarnam Church

Llanthony Church

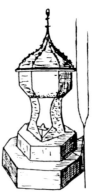

Llantilio Pertholey: font

Llantilio Crosseny Church

Tomb slab at Llanvetherine

LLANTILIO CROSSENNY   *St Teilo*   SO 399149

Patronage by the lords of White Castle on the hill above has resulted in a grander and more complex church than is usual for a village hereabouts. The central tower upon four narrow pointed arches is early 13th century. Four timbers support the frame of the ringing chamber inserted in 1708-9, when the broach-spire was rebuilt. The doorway over the west crossing arch gave access to the former rood loft. The nave of c1300 is aisled with arcades of four bays with double-chamfered arches on octagonal piers, although the scale is modest and the aisles are narrow. They have west lancets, and side windows of the 1850s. There is a spacious 14th century west porch. Openings high up suggest that there was a cell for a priest or hermit over the south transept, but this part is now roofed differently as a chapel. The north transept has been replaced by a wide 14th century north chapel extending along much of the chancel, and having towards it a fine arch (see the green man corbel on the west respond) evidently intended for a tomb, although no medieval monuments have survived. The chapel has a squint towards the main altar and an east window with ballflowers internally, although the tracery is a 15th century replacement. The chancel has east and SE windows with intersecting tracery of c1300, a cinquefoil-headed piscina, and one 14th century south window. There is a Norman tub font. The oldest monuments are to John Walderne and his family, once dated 1620, Charles Prosser and his wife, dated 1621, and Thomas Medlycott, d1738.

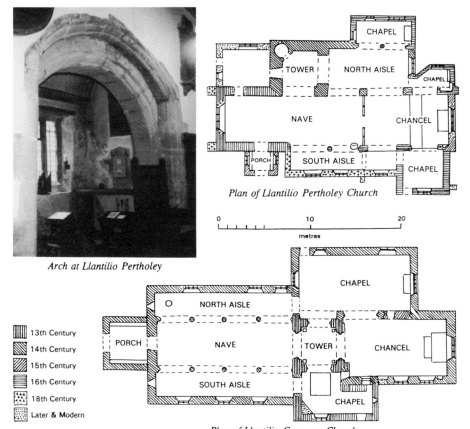

Arch at Llantilio Pertholey

Plan of Llantilio Pertholey Church

0   10   20

metres

13th Century

14th Century

15th Century

16th Century

18th Century

Later & Modern

Plan of Llantilio Crosseny Church

LLANTILIO PERTHOLEY   *St Teilo*   SO 312163

Some 13th century masonry may remain in the west half of the nave but the earliest datable parts are the tower set in the middle of the north side and the aisle extending from it to flank both the east bay of the nave and the west bay of the chancel, which are 14th century. The tower has arches to both nave and aisle and a stair in the NW corner. West of it now lies a meeting room of 1981. In the 15th century the porch was added and the chancel probably lengthened westwards. At the turn of the 15th and 16th centuries wagon roofs (repaired after a fire in 1974) were provided and a group of three chapels around the chancel. One forms a continuation of an early 16th century south aisle (the outer wall here was rebuilt in 1709). East of it is a larger chapel with an arch with timber responds. On the north is the peculiarly-shaped Neville Chapel with a stone rib-vault. Yet another chapel, with a two bay timber arcade, lies north of the north aisle. There is an octagonal 15th century font with fleur-de-llys on the base. The two early 16th century pews have been brought in from elsewhere. The west window of 1719 has contemporary texts painted on the splays. There is an old chest, and also an almsbox dated 1704. No medieval monuments remain but there are many 18th and 19th century tablets. See page 41.

Llantilio Pertholey Church

LLANTRISANT   *St Peter, St Paul and St John*   ST 391969

The chancel has one trefoil-headed south window of c1300. The west tower with a SE stair-turret, the south porch and one south window, and probably also the roodloft staircase projection (which is clearly an addition to the SE corner of the wide nave) are early 16th century, but two other windows could be 15th century. A tablet over the tower arch is dated 1593 and the octagonal font is dated 1673 with the name Iohn Iones. The oldest of the Kemys monuments is of Susanna, d1804.

LLANVACHES   *St Dyfrig*   ST 434916

The chancel and chancel arch were rebuilt in 1850 and 1862 respectively. The nave masonry also looks rebuilt but has old features such as two 14th century cusped lancets, the 17th century south doorway and door, and the blocked round-headed north doorway probably of c1500. The tower with a SE stair turret was begun about that time but the ashlar blocks change to rougher masonry higher up and the saddleback roof it ended up with cannot have been what was originally planned. The porch is also partly old and has a mortar serving as a stoup and part of a graveslab carved with a cock and other creatures. The octagonal font is 15th century.

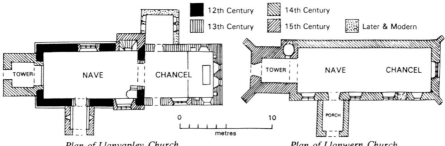

| ■ 12th Century | ▨ 14th Century |
| ▥ 13th Century | ▨ 15th Century | ▦ Later & Modern |

Plan of Llanvapley Church   *Plan of Llanwern Church*

LLANVAPLEY   *St Mabli*   SO 366141

The nave walls have a pronounced external batter and are probably Norman, the date of the font with chevrons around the rim. The 13th century chancel has a double piscina and two large east lancets and a cinquefoiled window above, all three being covered by a rere-arch internally. The west tower with a window with Y-tracery and an embattled and corbelled parapet is early 14th century. Two nave windows, one chancel window, and the ribbed wagon roofs are 15th century. The altar rails are dated 1724 and there is also an 18th century pulpit. Some of the tablets inside go back to the late 18th century.

LLANVETHERINE   *St James the Elder*   SO 364172

The belfry stage of the tower is corbelled out and has windows of three arched lights. It must be 16th century but the lower stages may be older, and the tower arch looks 14th century. The 14th century chancel has a piscina, east and south windows with cusped lights, an ogival-headed SW window, and the later roodloft staircase rising from its north wall. The nave has a fine 15th century south window of four cinquefoiled lights, and another window, and porch of that date, although there are signs of an earlier doorway over the inner doorway. A round-headed lancet dated 1703 lights the pulpit in the SE corner. The chancel arch is of 1872. The altar rails are 18th century. There is a low relief effigy of a medieval priest in the sanctuary. A foliated cross-slab is dated as late as 1601. There are reliefs of David Powell, d1621, a former fellow of All Souls at Oxford, and his wife, with the date 1715 added to the latter. There are several 18th century tablets signed by Thomas Brute. See page 46.

Llanvetherine Church   *Llanvaches Church*

LLANWENARTH   *St Peter*   SO 276148

Two nave north windows and the chancel with an ogival-headed priest's doorway and piscina, plus two windows with reticulated tracery, are 14th century, but the nave west lancet looks 13th century and clearly existed before a tower was inserted into the northern part of the west bay, leaving a peculiar little chamber south of it. The south porch and the ribbed wagon roof are 15th century and the south windows are of 1853 or 1877. There is a Norman tub font.

LLANWERN   *St Mary*   ST 371879

This is a late 14th century single chamber with a three-light window and diagonal buttresses at the east end, where there is a piscina, and a south porch of the same build. The diagonally buttressed west tower with a NE stair-turret is a 15th century addition. Inside is the head of a pre-Norman cross. See page 42.

LOWER MACHEN   *St Michael*   ST 228881

The unusually wide nave is probably 13th century since there is a lancet now looking into the embattled tower, and there are recesses on either side of the chancel arch of undressed stone. The porch is late medieval and so is the tower west doorway, although the walls may be older and the belfry openings could be later. All the other windows are of the 1900-1 restoration by C.B.Fowler. A classically moulded arch in the chancel north wall leads into a square mausoleum of c1716 in which are many monuments to various branches of the Morgan family, including John (of Ruperra), d1715, John & Martha, d1719 & 1720, Sir William, d1731, Charles & John, d1787 & 1792. There are eleven hatchments dating from 1767 to 1867, early 19th century royal arms, and a tiny font which is probably 18th century.

Magor Church

MAGOR   *St Mary*   ST 425869

St Cadwalader, the last Welsh ruler to consider himself as King of Britain, is said to have founded a church here in the 7th century. Stones with chevrons reset on the chancel are relics of a Norman church here dedicated to St Leonard. The central tower is 13th century, with plain pointed arches of that date towards the nave and chancel. The tower has a square NW stair turret and later belfry windows and a plain corbelled parapet. There are arcades of three bays but the embattled aisles of c1500 have a fourth bay beside the tower, with wave-mouldings on the arches cut through the tower north and south walls. The windows were all renewed by John Norton in 1861-8, and he provided a completely new east window for the 14th century chancel. There is a fine rib-vaulted north porch with diagonal buttresses, a pierced parapet, an image niche over the inner doorway, and an upper room. The porch and the narrower part of the north aisle from which it projects are relics of an earlier 15th century layout with narrower aisles. The arcade piers have capitals in the form of angels holding scrolls. On the south side the western pier has a green man corbel, and the eastern pier has a image niche. The octagonal 15th century font has double-cusped arcading and faces with hollow chamfers. Beside it is a large foliage boss from a vault. There are ruins of a 16th century priest's house beside the churchyard.

Plan of Magor Church

Lower Machen Church

Llanwenarth Church

Mamhilad Church

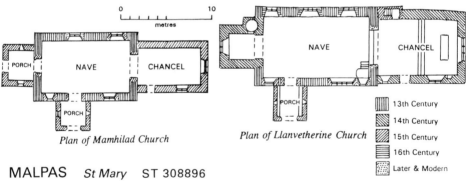

Plan of Mamhilad Church

Plan of Llanvetherine Church

13th Century
14th Century
15th Century
16th Century
Later & Modern

MALPAS *St Mary* ST 308896

Just one head corbel in the vestry remains of the original church founded here c1110 to serve a cell of the Cluniac priory of Montacute in Somerset. The existing neo-Norman church is of 1849-50 by John Pritchard. The elaborate west doorway and chancel arch are similar to (if not copies of) the Norman originals.

MAMHILAD *St Illtyd* SO 305034

The features of the nave and chancel are mostly 15th century, although there is evidence of older masonry, especially on the north side. The west and south porches and the chancel arch and the much renewed screen across are also 15th century, the date 1482 having been found on plaster in the south porch during Pritchard and Seddon's restoration of 1864-5. Part of the former loft has been reused in the west gallery. Parts of the stained glass in the east window are medieval. The font looks like a Norman tub later remodelled to fit onto a panelled base.

Marshfield Church

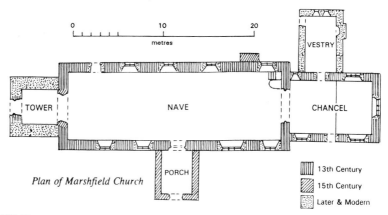

Plan of Marshfield Church

13th Century
15th Century
Later & Modern

MARSHFIELD *St Mary* ST 262826

This was once a fine early 13th century church built under patronage by St Augustine's Abbey at Bristol and employing the same craftsmen that worked at Llandaff Cathedral. The battered plinth on the unusually wide and long nave was topped by a moulding which has been hacked off. The round-arched south doorway has one order of shafts with stiffleaf capitals and the arch has a roll decorated with chevrons set across it. The chancel arch, which is pointed, also has one order of shafts. Reset in the west wall of the embattled and rebuilt 15th century tower is another 13th century doorway with two filleted rolls. It probably came from the chancel south wall when that part was rebuilt in the 15th century. The windows of that period have all been restored, and a north vestry was added in 1866. The tower arch is tall and narrow and has wave-mouldings. The 15th century porch has fleurons in the finely moulded outer arch and a floriated cross-slab is set into its wall.

MATHERN   *St Tewdric*   ST 524908

The church and the palace of the bishops of Llandaff lie together at the end of a lane beyond the village. The church resembles those of western England, mainly because of two campaigns during the bishopric from 1478 to 1496 of John Marshall. Firstly he widened the aisles, providing three-light windows on both sides and in the end walls, and adding a porch, and then he added an ashlar-faced west tower of three stages with a polygonal stair-turret, battlements and corner pinnacles. All these parts have diagonal corner buttresses and there are coupled intermediate buttresses on the north side. Fragments of stained glass of this period are gathered together in the south aisle west window. Squints from the aisles look into the 13th century chancel with a double piscina, one north lancet and a set of three on the east which internally are set under one arch with a roll-moulding. Also 13th century are the piers of the four bay arcades, lozenge-shaped with shafts at the cardinal points. On the south side the arches may be a 15th century replacement. On the north side there are three double-chamfered arches and then a 12th century pier with a 15th century arch between it and the respond. The discovery of the base of a similar pier 3.7m further north during restoration suggested the possibility that there was a narrow Norman aisled nave where the north aisle now is. A disused font in the north aisle has the date 1705 scratched upon it. The worn incised slab in the middle of the chancel floor is said to mark the burial place of the heart and bowels of Bishop Miles Salley, d1516. A tomb slab in the nave bears a bishop's staff in relief. On the south aisle wall is a brass depicting Philip and Alice Williams, d1562 & 1567. There are many 19th century tablets to the Williams family and one also to Thomas Hughes, d1667.

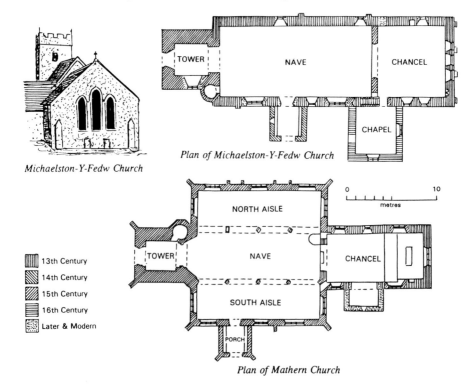

Michaelston-Y-Fedw Church

TOWER   NAVE   CHANCEL

CHAPEL

Plan of Michaelston-Y-Fedw Church

0   10
metres

|||| 13th Century
\\\\ 14th Century
//// 15th Century
≡ 16th Century
▨ Later & Modern

NORTH AISLE

TOWER   NAVE   CHANCEL

SOUTH AISLE

PORCH

Plan of Mathern Church

Michaelston-y-Fedw Church

MICHAELSTON-Y-FEDW

St Michael ST 241846

The wide 13th century nave and chancel are the same width and may have been undivided until the existing chancel arch was built later. There are several wide lancets, some of them restored, and a set of three in the east wall. One north window embrasure has traces of old paintings. There are three pilaster buttresses along the north side and four (the outer ones gabled) on the east wall. There are two blocked doorways in the chancel north wall, one possibly a relic of a Norman church. The embattled west tower with pinnacles, a SE stair-turret, and a west doorway with a wave-moulding, is 15th century, and probably also so is the nave wagon-roof. Placed on the south side so as to look both into the nave and chancel is the mid 16th century chapel of the Kemeys family of Cefn Mabli. It has square-headed windows with arched lights facing south and east and contains a tablet to Mary and Anne Kemeys, d1708, and an early 17th century monument. The font with the bowl encased in leaves and a tree for a stem with an entwined serpent is 18th century.

Mathern Church

Mitchel Troy Church

Doorway at St Thomas, Monmouth

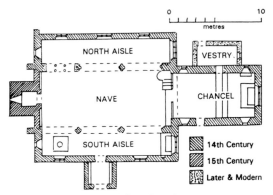

Plan of Mitchel Troy Church

Old print of St Thomas, Monmouth

MITCHEL TROY St Michael SO 493104

This 14th century church was slightly grander than most of its neighbours, with aisles of three bays with a double sunk quadrant moulding on the arches and piers of the arcades. The south aisle east window has three cusped lancets stepping down under a head sloped like that of the aisle roof. There are cusped lancets in the aisle west walls and in the chancel, although the latter was rebuilt in 1873-6 by John Pritchard, when the north vestry was added. He also rebuilt the north aisle, which had been damaged by the collapse of the spire in the 18th century, modified one bay of the arcade to fit in the organ, and provided the corbelled top stage on the tiny west tower. On the SW corner of the tower is an inscription asking for prayers on behalf of Godfrey and Joanne, and there was formerly a date of 1414. There is a Norman tub font. The cross shaft in the churchyard has shields and ballflowers on the angles. Notable rectors here were Adam of Usk in 1382, and Nathaniel Baxter in 1602.

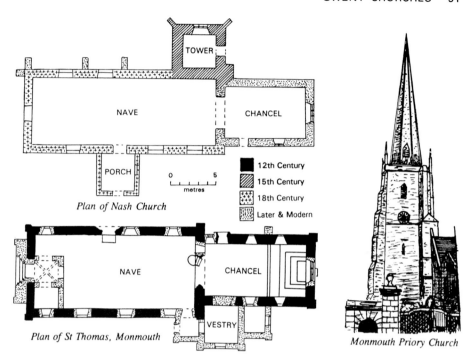

Plan of Nash Church

12th Century
15th Century
18th Century
Later & Modern

Plan of St Thomas, Monmouth

Monmouth Priory Church

MONMOUTH *St Mary* ST 509130

Only the late 14th century west tower remains of the Benedictine priory church founded c1080 and consecrated in 1101. The choir became a ruin after the Dissolution and the nave was demolished in 1732 and replaced in 1736-7 by a new aisled building with the old tower attached to its north aisle. The tower top stage and spire are a rebuilding of c1740 by Nathaniel Wilkinson. In the 1880s the Georgian church was remodelled with new six-bay arcades and a new east end added to a design by G.E.Street. The heavy buttresses flanking the tower originally formed part of the 11th century west front and the position of the Norman south arcade is marked by a round respond now almost centrally placed on the inside of the west wall. In the south aisle are a collection of 13th and 15th century tiles, one being dated 1465. There is a fine set of Kempe stained glass windows. The oldest monuments are to Elizabeth Mynors, d1707, and John Hoskyns, d1715, in the south aisle and to Henry Allen, d1767, and Joseph Price, d1796 in the north aisle.

MONMOUTH *St Thomas Becket* ST 505124

The suburb of Overmonnow, just beyond the river bridge to the SW, has its own Norman church on the riverbank. The nave was mostly rebuilt in 1830-1 (when a neo-Norman font imitating those of the Herefordshire school was provided), and made even more Norman than before by an impressive west doorway of 1880. Both parts have original north doorways, with chevrons on that in the chancel, where two original windows remain on each side, together with pilasters clasping the corners. Although its impost shafts are renewed, the chancel arch with a hoodmould, roll and chevrons is original. A second, octagonal, font is 15th century.

MOUNTON   *St Andoenus*   ST 512929

This small nave and chancel church between a lane and a cliff edge was mostly rebuilt in 1880 by Walter Evill. It has a tablet to William Hollis, d1799.

MYNYDDISLWYN

St Tudor   ST 194939

The church lies by a pub on a bare hilltop. The embattled west tower with a NE stair-turret is 15th century. The rest was rebuilt c1820 as single chamber with a wide north aisle extending almost as far east. No old furnishings remain.

NASH   *St Mary*   ST 344837

The only medieval part is the late 15th century diagonally buttressed tower with a tall spire built at the expense of Eton College, holders of the rectory since 1450. The tower lies in a north transeptal position but never functioned as a transept since it did not communicate with the rest of the church. Its west wall has the roof line of a north aisle demolished in 1792, when the present ceiling, west gallery, box pews and pulpit were installed. The nave south wall and porch are earlier 18th century work, whilst the chancel was rebuilt by Seddon in 1861. See pp51&55.

NEWCHURCH   *St Peter*

ST   454976

The tiny 14th century west tower with a trefoiled lancet over a blocked west doorway has had a SE stair turret added to it later. The north doorway and porch are 15th century. There is also a disused early tub font. The other features date from J.P.Seddon's restoration of 1863-4, when a south vestry was added.

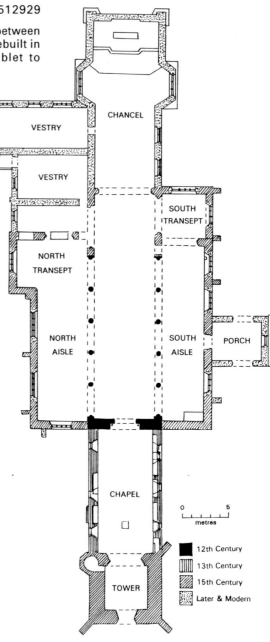

Plan of Newport Cathedral

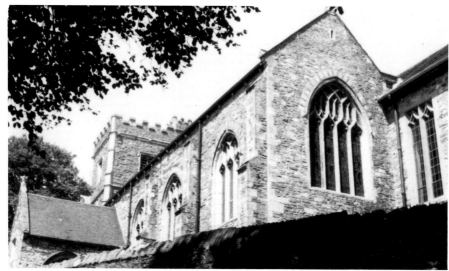

Newport Cathedral

NEWPORT   *St Woolos*   ST 309876

The church lies on a high promontory and can only be approached from the west. It was founded as a timber structure in the 6th century by a Welsh chieftain of Wentloog called Gwynllyw (Woolos in English). A later stone church was plundered in turn by Irish pirates, the Danes, and the English in the 1050s under Harold Godwinson. It was destroyed by Caradoc, Lord of Caerleon, but was rebuilt after being granted by William Rufus (William II of England) to Gloucester Abbey. The nave built c1120 was rebuilt in the 13th century with three lancets on each side and a number of tomb recesses, and has become a galilee chapel of St Mary. The lancets were reinstated as such in 1913, after being opened out as larger windows in 1818. West of St Mary's chapel is a large diagonally buttressed west tower with a polygonal NE stair-turret. On the south side is a shield with a Tudor rose and the headless statue is probably of Jasper Tudor, Lord of Newport for the ten years following his nephew Henry VII's victory at Bosworth in 1485. A very fine chevron adorned arch of c1180 with one order of shafts with richly carved capitals leads through the east wall of the galilee chapel into a mid 12th century aisled nave of five bays. The arcades have round arches of two orders on circular piers with scalloped capitals, and there are original clerestory windows immediately above the arches. After being burnt by Owain Glyndwr in 1402 the aisles were rebuilt wider, a transept of slightly greater projection was formed on the north, and the nave given a new wagon roof. The large three and four light windows on each side and the large south porch were rebuilt during restoration of 1853. A chancel mostly of that date was swept away by a large new choir of 1960-4, the church having become the cathedral of a new diocese formed in 1921. There are spacious new vestries to the north of it.

The font in St Mary's Chapel is partly 12th century and partly of 1854. Here are damaged effigies of a crosslegged knight of c1300, a early 14th century lady, Sir Walter Herbert of St Julians, d1568, and parts of a late 15th century knight and lady, perhaps Sir John Morgan of Tredegar, d1493, whose arms appear on a panel nearby. The oldest of the many tablets in the aisles is to Mary James, d1792.

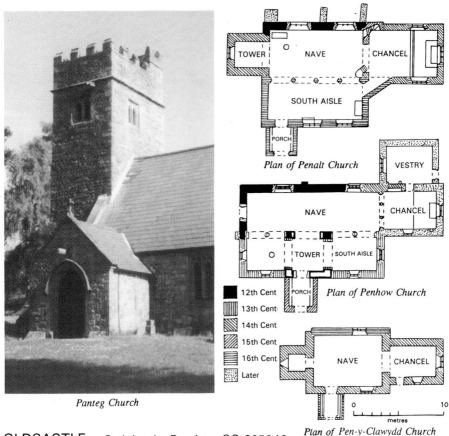

Plan of Penalt Church

Plan of Penhow Church

12th Cent
13th Cent
14th Cent
15th Cent
16th Cent
Later

0   10
metres

Plan of Pen-y-Clawydd Church

Panteg Church

OLDCASTLE   *St John the Baptist*   SO 325246

Now lying derelict, this church was rebuilt on the old foundations by Seddon in 1863-4. Three Norman windows remain on the north side.

PANTEG   *St Mary*   ST 311910

Only the small embattled 15th century west tower with a NE stair-turret survived the rebuilding of the nave in 1849 and the addition of a new chancel, north aisle and L-shaped series of north vestries by Henry Woodyer in 1874-6.

PENALT   *Dedication Unknown*   ST 523107

The church lies alone, perched above the River Wye. The nave north wall is perhaps 12th century and the chancel is probably 14th century, as is the saddleback roofed west tower. The south aisle with a four bay arcade, the squint passage through to the chancel, and the chancel windows may all be of 1539, the date that appears on the south door with a porch in front. However the roodloft staircase must be slightly earlier and perhaps also the wagon roofs. The nave north windows are of 1885. A tablet near the pulpit dates it to 1634 and the octagonal font may also be 17th century. There are royal arms of Queen Anne dated 1709 and altar rails dated 1743.

PENHOW   *St John the Baptist*   St 424908

The pyramidal-roofed tower lies on the south side of what is thought to be a Norman nave, and has a 15th century porch in front of it. The tower is older than the short lengths of 13th century aisle each with two bay arcades on circular piers, so it is likely to be of c1200. The chancel was mostly rebuilt in 1913 by H.J.Griggs, when a north vestry was added, but it has a 13th century double piscina and an ogival-headed 14th century tomb recess in the north wall.

PENRHOS   *St Cadoc*   SO 416117

The chancel has two windows of 14th century type and is probably an addition to an earlier nave. Both parts have late medieval windows of two or three cinquefoil-headed lights and ribbed wagon roofs, and two other windows of that period are reset at each end of the three bay north aisle added along with the south porch in 1878 by John Pritchard. The west tower with a corbelled and embattled top stage is probably 16th century, although the tower arch could be earlier.

PENTERRY   *St Mary*   ST 520988

This small single chamber lying alone in a field above the Wye was mostly rebuilt in 1853-61 by Pritchard & Seddon, but one small Norman window remains on the north side and there is a square-headed 15th century east window of two lights.

Tower at Nash

Penhow Church

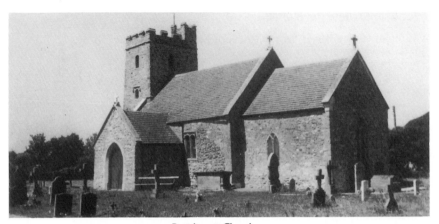

Portskewett Church

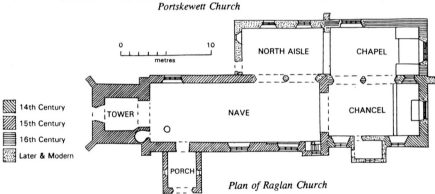

14th Century
15th Century
16th Century
Later & Modern

NORTH AISLE   CHAPEL

TOWER   NAVE   CHANCEL

PORCH

Plan of Raglan Church

PEN-Y-CLAWYDD   *St Martin*   SO 452079

The pyramidal roof and top part of the west tower and the timber-framed porch date from the restoration of 1885 which has left one cusped ogival-headed 14th century window in the chancel as the only dating evidence. The whole church could be of that date (see the renewed chancel arch), although the nave has been very slightly widened to the north. The worn slab with a bust of a man emerging from a floriated cross could be slightly earlier, and the tub font is Norman. See page 54.

PETERSTONE WENTLOOG   *St Peter*   ST 268801

As a result of patronage by St Augustine's Abbey at Bristol this is the finest 15th century church in Gwent, despite the rebuilding of the chancel (and probably also the north aisle) in 1889-91. The aisles do not reach quite to the diagonally buttressed west tower, leaving a very short section of unaisled nave as in many Devon churches. The tower is embattled with pinnacles on the corners and a NE stair turret. In niches on the parapet are figures of St Mary, St James, St John and St Peter. There are vine-leaves in the hollows of the west doorway mouldings. The arcades are of four bays with piers with filleted shafts, with minor shafts in the diagonals. There is a hammerbeam roof supported on head corbels. The south aisle has a piscina, three-light windows, and a large porch.

Pen-y-Clawydd Church

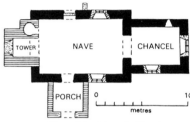

Plan of Portskewett Church

Peterstone Wentloog Church

PORTSKEWETT   *St Mary*   ST 499882

The nave has north and south doorways with huge lintels, that on the north having a Greek cross set in a semicircle, and a plain round chancel arch. The chancel has one Norman window on the north and a two-light window with Y-tracery of c1300 on the south, whilst the east window is 19th century. There is also a 14th century south window in the nave. The west tower with a blocked west doorway, a NE stair-turret, and square-hoodmoulded belfry windows is early 16th century. The west gallery of 1818 is lighted by a window high up on the north. On the octagonal 15th century font are carved quatrefoils, blind arcading, and a four-petalled flower.

RAGLAN   *St Cadoc*   SO 414076

In the very thick south wall of the chancel are a pair of early 14th century windows with cusped Y-tracery. The nave with its south porch, roodloft staircase (now giving access to the pulpit), and several restored windows is 15th century. The fine diagonally buttressed west tower with panelled battlements and corner pinnacles is thought to be an addition of the 1460s. The founder of the castle has his effigy at Abergavenny but it passed to the Somersets in the 16th century they added a chapel on the north side with a two bay arcade towards the chancel. It contains effigies of the third and fourth earls of Worcester, William, d1589, and Edward, d1628, and the latter's wife Elizabeth, all much damaged by the Parliamentarians in 1646. There are two old chests, one dated 1677, in T.H.Wyatt's western extension of 1867 of the chapel, forming a north aisle to the nave. Part of the 15th century font also remains.

REDWICK   *St Thomas*   ST 413841

The lower part of the central tower may be Norman. The arches to the nave and chancel are 14th century, as are the arcades of three bays of double-chamfered arches on octagonal piers, the aisles, and the chancel. The south aisle has an ogival-headed piscina. There was another remodelling in the 15th century which provided the tower top, the roodloft stair in the south aisle, the large south porch with an image niche over the outer arch, several windows and the worn west doorway with fleurons in the mouldings. The west front was otherwise mostly rebuilt by John Norton in 1874-5, when an immersion font was inserted in the south aisle. The rood loft contains some old parts but is mostly of 1948. See page 7.

RISCA   *St Mary*   ST 236912

When the medieval church was demolished in 1852 part of a circular building, thought to be Roman, was revealed below it. The existing church with aisles and a south tower with a spire is by W.G. and E. Habershon.

ROCKFIELD   *St Cenedlon*   SO 482148

Only the octagonal font with blank traceried panels, the arms of William III dated 1700, a few loose carved pieces from the screen now in the vestry, and the west tower with a recessed timber upper stage survived the rebuilding of 1959-60 by Pritchard and Seddon. The church has a north aisle and a north vestry.

ROGIET   *St Mary*   ST 457876

The 14th century chancel has trefoiled lancets on each side and an east window with reticulated tracery. The short nave, the south porch and the diagonally buttressed west tower with a SE stair-turret capped by a spirelet are 15th century. The north aisle and north vestry were added in 1903. The chancel is probably Norman. The church of Llanfihangel Rogiet lies very close to the west and there was a third church at Ifton, 1km to the east, until it was demolished c1755.

RUNSTON   *St Kenya*

ST 495916

The village has gone, leaving just one farm and the Norman chapel which has been ruinous since the 18th century. It has a narrow chancel arch, north and south doorways, and several narrow windows, all with round heads, except that some are now just robbed-out gaps. At the west end a modest turret stands within footings of a never-completed tower. There was never any east window.

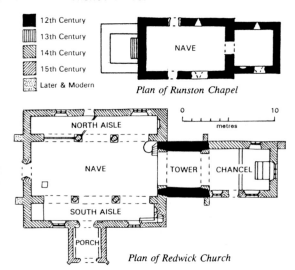

12th Century
13th Century
14th Century
15th Century
Later & Modern

Plan of Runston Chapel

NAVE

NORTH AISLE

NAVE

TOWER   CHANCEL

SOUTH AISLE

PORCH

0   metres   10

Plan of Redwick Church

Runston Chapel

ST ARVANS   *St Arvan*   ST 517965

The priest's doorway with crosses in boxes is Early Norman, and east of it are paired 13th century lancets. The rest of the church is of 1883-4 by John Pritchard, although there is a 10th century cross fragment with interlace built into a north aisle window. There is also a worn 14th or 15th century effigy on a south aisle window-sill.

ST BRIDES NETHERWENT   *St Bridget*   ST 428896

The village was abandoned in the 18th century and the north aisle of the church was allowed to collapse in 1790 and the south aisle in 1812. In 1848 the nave was rebuilt without aisles, a porch added, and the chancel remodelled. As a result the only medieval parts are the goblet-shaped Norman font and the low saddleback-roofed west tower of c1300 with twin lancets below and a single one above facing north.

St Arvans Church

ST BRIDES WENTLOOG   *St Bridget*   ST 293824

This church amongst the marshes by the Severn Estuary was rescued from dereliction in 1995-7, when the tower arch and two bay north arcade with niches on the piers were opened up again. All the ancient features are 15th century but not of one campaign. The diagonally buttressed west tower is very fine although part of the panelled parapet, the angle pinnacles, and two of the crowning images are missing. However the Trinity still remains on the east side and the Virgin and Child on the south side, where there is another image in a niche lower down. The chancel is small compared with the long and wide nave. Both have original windows, several with hoodmoulds on headstops. The porch has what looks like a Norman window reset over the outer entrance. The nave and aisle have original boarded wagon roofs.

ST MAUGHANS   *St Meugan*   SO 461171

The church is double-naved, unusual for this part of Wales, with an arcade of octagonal timber piers supporting a huge moulded beam which may be late 16th century. The wagon roofs must also be of that period. The northern nave is 13th century with north lancets and a Y-traceried east window, and the arcade west respond suggests there was already a south aisle then, although it must have been widened subsequently, and then, since there is a joint in the south wall, later extended the full length of the church. The porch is dated 1732 on the keystone. The west tower may also be 13th century although its timber framed upper stage is of 1865, the date on the weather-vane. There is a Norman tub font.

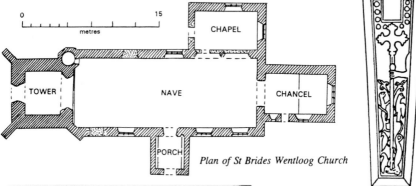

Plan of St Brides Wentloog Church

St Pierre: graveslab

St Maughans Church

Window at St Maughans

ST PIERRE   *St Peter*   ST 515905

The church lies close to the house of the Lewis family, now a hotel. The nave is Norman, with one original north window and herringbone masonry visible internally. A chancel the same width as the nave was added in the early 14th century and retains one trefoiled lancet. The north doorway and porch with a crocketed and pinnacled niche over the outer arch is 14th or 15th century. One south window is 15th century but the others are of 1843 and 1874. The octagonal font and the screen are also 15th century. There are floriated cross slabs to a priest (possibly William Benet, d1240), and Urien de St Pierre, who was alive in 1273. The priest's cross has birds and dragons on the shaft and is held by a hand.

SHIRENEWTON   *St Thomas Becket*   ST 478935

The central tower with corbelled battlements and a cinquefoiled window on the south is 14th century. The chancel is mostly rebuilt but has a 15th century priest's doorway. The nave and two storey south porch are also rather renewed and a north aisle with a three bay arcade was added in 1852-3. The west front has a tiger-head water-spout and there are two human-headed gargoyles on the tower parapet.

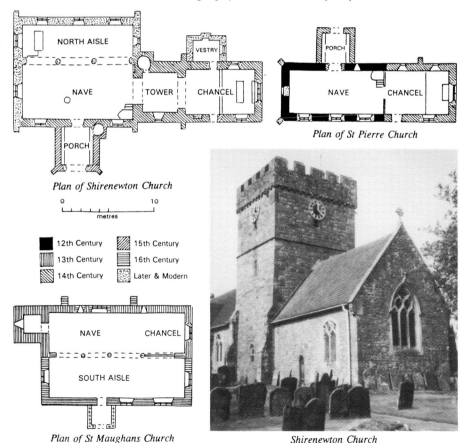

Plan of St Pierre Church

Plan of Shirenewton Church

0   10
metres

- 12th Century
- 13th Century
- 14th Century
- 15th Century
- 16th Century
- Later & Modern

Plan of St Maughans Church

Shirenewton Church

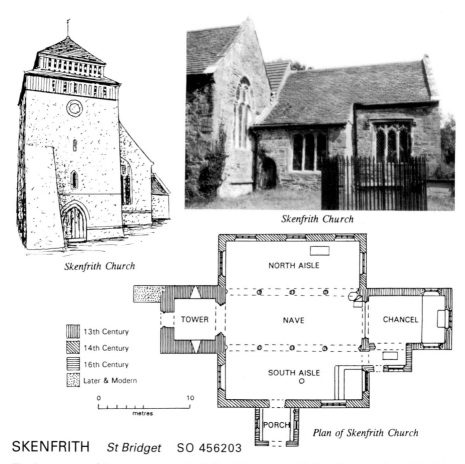

Skenfrith Church

Skenfrith Church

NORTH AISLE

TOWER   NAVE   CHANCEL

13th Century

14th Century

16th Century

Later & Modern

0   10

metres

SOUTH AISLE

PORCH   *Plan of Skenfrith Church*

SKENFRITH   *St Bridget*   SO 456203

The lower part of the west tower, the fully aisled nave with four bay arcades of double-chamfered arches on circular piers, and the chancel are all 13th century, just as one might expect with an important castle of that date nearby. There is dogtooth on the capital of the southern respond of the chancel arch. The aisles were later rebuilt wider, the north aisle having early 14th century windows, as has the chancel (where the east window has fragments of old glass), whilst the south aisle has late 14th century windows, including a square-headed one of four lights facing south. The south porch and vestry are 16th century and the timber-framed tower top with a recessed upper stage with a pyramidal roof is probably also of that date. The aisle roofs are old, and the wall plate in the north aisle is dated 1663. The church has escaped much restoration and has much of interest inside. The font and chest are both dated 1661 and the altar rails with turned balusters are not much later. The reading desk contains old panels, probably from a former screen. There are medieval pews in the north aisle, and also some 17th century box-pews. Painted inscriptions of the 16th and 17th centuries remain here and there. In the north aisle are an altar tomb with an incised slab depicting Sir John Morgan, d1557, last governor of the Three Castles, and a 15th century red cope of embroidered velvet with saints under canopies, the Virgin and Child, three seraphim, and two double-headed eagles.

STANTON   *Dedication Unknown*   SO 311213

A chapel of c1400 which served a grange of Llanthony Abbey has been converted into a cowshed. Three ogival-headed windows still remain.

SUDBROOKE   *Holy Trinity*   ST 507873

The Norman church below the rampart of the coastal hillfort is mostly reduced to foundations except for the nave west wall with one 14th century cinquefoil-headed lancet, the 14th century chancel arch on plain imposts, and the arch of the late medieval south porch. The chancel was enlarged in the 14th century.

TINTERN   *St Mary*   SO 530999

A steep cobble path leads up to a church which was mostly rebuilt by John Pritchard in 1866-8 when the saddleback-roofed north tower was added. The rest of the building was unroofed in 1973. The windows are 14th century in style.

TINTERN PARVA   *St Michael*   SO 532007

The font with pyramidal base spurs is 13th century, and the vaulted south porch is 15th century. The rest of the church was mostly rebuilt in 1846-7 and remodelled in 1889. One old cross-slab remains on the floor.

TREDUNNOCK   *St Andrew*   ST 380949

The small nave and chancel both have small Norman windows but are on different axes. The short west tower is probably 14th century with a later embattled top. One south window, the priest's doorway, and the south doorway and porch with its original roof are 15th century. The font is dated 1662 and near it is a Roman tombstone to Julius Julianus (of the 2nd Augustan Legion) dug up in 1680.

Tredunnock Church

TREGARE   *St Mary*   SO 417102

The 14th century nave has an ogival headed south doorway and a fine north window of two lights with a quatrefoil under the ogival head and keeled shafting to the embrasure inside. A similar west window was cut down and the tracery removed to make an arch into the tower, which has a pyramidal roof with a large weathercock and 19th century openings. The chancel arch is surmounted by another arch above it. One window with twin lancets in the chancel could be 13th century but the square windows there appear to be of 1638, the year that appears on one of them. The plain mullioned south window in the nave is probably 16th century. Both nave and chancel have late medieval roofs. In the chancel is a monument to John Evans, d1704.

TRELLECK   *St Nicholas*   SO 501055

Most of the existing church dates from soon after the Welsh burnt the town, newly founded by the de Clares, in 1296. The round-arched priest's doorway is the only possible older feature. The building now seems too large for the present small village. The church has an aisled nave of five bays with octagonal piers and a clerestory, a west tower, and a chancel the same width as the nave which was partly rebuilt in 1893-4, when the chancel arch was slightly heightened. The ashlar-faced tower has a four-light west window with cusped reticulated tracery over a doorway, and a spire with four gabled lucarnes which is recessed behind a parapet. It is flanked by rooms which presumably were intended as vestries, as they are now, since they only have west facing windows and are entered through modest doorways rather than any piercing of the tower north and south walls. The aisles have wide cusped lancets divided by buttresses and with cusped rere-arches on the north side, and the east windows are of three lights with the middle one cusped. In the chancel are early 17th century altar rails, a worn effigy of a priest and an ogival-headed piscina. There is a more ornate piscina in the south aisle. The pulpit is of 1639, that date being on a panel behind the reading desk, and there are carved and coloured royal arms of Charles II dated 1683. The south porch may be as late as 1595, the date appearing on the south door. In the west end of the south aisle is the head of a sundial set up by Lady Magdalen Probert in 1689 with incised flowers and reliefs showing the castle mound, the prehistoric Harold's Stones, and the Virtuous Holy Well (1 km to the SE).

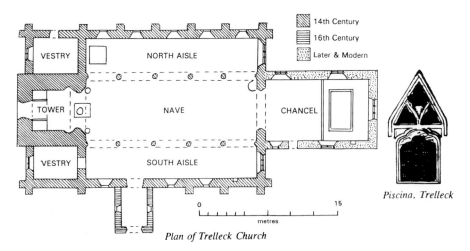

Plan of Trelleck Church

Piscina, Trelleck

TRELLECK GRANGE   *Dedication Unknown*   SO 492017

This small single chamber was much restored in 1860-1.

TREVETHIN   *St Cadoc*   SO 284020

Only the 15th century west tower with a NE stair-turret survived the rebuilding of the church (with transepts, a north aisle and large north vestry) in 1846-7 for the Hanburys of Pontypool Park. The oldest of the several Hanbury monuments are to John, d1734, Capel, d1765, and John, d1795. Tablets to others lie in the nave.

TROSTREY   *St David*   SO 360044

The single chamber lies alone high above the Usk. The three-light east window, the other windows of two lights, the west doorway and porch, and the screen with a stair up to the former loft are all 15th century. The north windows are of the restoration of 1872 when the wagon roof was mostly renewed. The font is thought to be a late medieval panelled base now set upside down as the bowl and placed upon the original 12th century bowl also set upside down. There is a monument with a broken segmental pediment to Charles Hughes, d1676. There is also an old chest.

UNDY   *St Mary*   ST 440869

The windows were renewed or replaced in 1880 by John Pritchard, when a belfry was placed over the chancel arch. This arch appears to reuse parts from a former arch into an early tower at the nave east end which is said to have been dismantled c1860. The west window was of c1300, the east window early 16th century, and the chancel south windows 15th century. Also 15th century is the fine doorway with a hoodmould on head-stops oddly placed at the south end of the west wall. The porch is dated 1790 but looks older. The 13th century font has a square bowl upon a circular stem with four attached circular shafts.

Gravestone at Trelleck

Tower doorway at Trelleck

Niche bracket at Usk

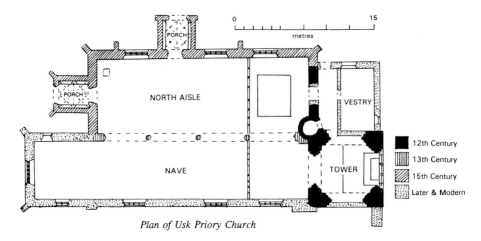

0   15
metres

PORCH

PORCH

NORTH AISLE

VESTRY

NAVE

TOWER

■ 12th Century

▦ 13th Century

▨ 15th Century

▦ Later & Modern

Plan of Usk Priory Church

USK   *St Mary*   SO 379008

This church originally served a Benedictine nunnery founded by Richard de Clare (Strongbow) shortly after Usk was recovered from the Welsh in 1174. From that time there remain only the font with chamfered corners and the central tower with round-arched belfry windows and a circular NW stair turret. Three of the crossing arches were blocked up when the monastic choir and transepts were demolished after the Dissolution, although the north blocking has been pierced by a doorway to a vestry. After years of secular use the tower was restored to the church in 1844 and a sanctuary formed below it. The nave was then rebuilt and lengthened by one wide bay to the west. Before also taking over the nave at the Dissolution the townsfolk used a north aisle added in the 13th century with an arcade of four wide bays with circular piers. The eastern pier also has four attached shafts. The aisle was rebuilt much wider c1460 by Sir William Herbert and has rib-vaulted west and north porches with image niches over their doorways. The fine screen across both aisle and nave is of about the same period. Fixed upon it is a brass inscription in Welsh commemorating the celebrated chronicler Adam of Usk, c1365-1430. The four-light windows were restored in 1899-1900. The pulpit (originally a three decker) and altar rails are 18th century. The monuments include a gravestone to Walter Jones, d1656, and a draped urn to Samuel Browne, d1790, signed by Tyley of Bristol. There is also a very worn 14th century effigy lying outside near the west porch.

WHITSON   *Dedication Unknown*   ST 381834

The south doorway with rolls on the arch and foliage capitals on the shafts, and the font with a band of lattice ornamentation are both Norman. The 15th century tower leans to the south. The chancel, south porch and nave windows date from 1861. There are several tablets to the Phillips family of Whitson Court, the builder of which, William, died in 1789 in his 101st year.

WILCRICK   *St Mary*   ST 410880

The restoration of 1860 has left a plastered late medieval wagon roof in the nave, a Norman font, a datestone of 1621 in the east wall, and a set of late 17th or 18th century altar rails with turned balusters.

Trelleck Church

Usk Priory Church

WOLVESNEWTON   *St Thomas Becket*   ST 454998

A probably 13th century nave was lengthened westwards in the 15th century and given two new doorways, that on the south having a porch (the northern one is now blocked). The chancel is probably 15th century, although its features are of the 1855-7 restoration by John Norton. The saddleback-roofed tower may be 16th century. The war memorial in front of the church uses part of a medieval cross.

WONASTOW   *St Wonnow*   SO 486107

The church lies hidden behind Wonastow Court. The chancel has 15th century square-headed windows of two lights facing north, east and south, and there is the very unusual feature of a north facing priest's doorway. The almost square nave is of 1863 (the west tower is dated 1865), and the north porch is of 1909. The chancel has early 20th century furnishings and a monument to George Milborne, d1637.

GAZETTEER OF GLAMORGAN CHURCHES

ABERDARE   *St John*   SO 000027

The triple roll-moulded south doorway and the nave masonry are of c1300 and the arch-braced roof (now boarded over) is partly late medieval. The chancel was rebuilt in 1777 and is said to have been enlarged in 1871-6 (the date of the nave windows and porch) but it seems too small for that to be possible. There is a square-headed double bellcote. The medieval octagonal font has a roll at the top and bottom.

ABERPERGWM   *St Cadoc*   SN 870062

There was a medieval church here in the grounds of ruined Aberpergwm House but it was rebuilt in 1808, remodelled in 1840 for William Williams, and again altered in 1883. The medieval effigies under arches in the east wall are probably from France.

BAGLAN   *St Baglan*   SS 753923

Further up the hill from St Catherine's church of 1875-82 is the medieval church, a ruin since a fire in 1954. The western half may be 12th century but the east half, with a three light east window is 15th century. Of the three blocked south windows the easternmost is 16th century work of three lights under a square head.

BARRY ISLAND   *St Baruch*   ST 119666

In an enclosure beside the holiday camp entrance are the foundations of a tiny nave and apse of c1140 with traces of a priest's house close by on the north. A small medieval church of St Nicholas in the town (at 105674) was demolished in 1872.

BEDWAS   *St Barrwg*   ST 172892

The church lies on a slope above the Rhymney. The nave has a pointed-arched south doorway approached by steps. It and the porch and chancel are all probably 13th century although the windows are of the restoration of 1875 by John Pritchard, when the north chapel was rebuilt. The saddleback-roofed tower with gables facing north and south has a west doorway with a shouldered lintel surmounted by a window with Y-tracery, suggesting a date c1300. The circular font is probably Norman.

Aberdare Church

Baglan Old Church

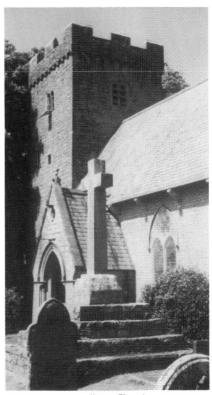

BETWS   *St David*   SS 899867

The most interesting feature is the double bellcote on corbelling with a pyramidal cap. The round-headed doorway suggests a possible Norman date for the nave, but it and the chancel have late medieval roofs and the priest's doorway is also of that period. The windows all date from G.E.Halliday's restoration of 1893, when the north aisle and NE vestry were added. The only old furnishing is a tub-shaped font.

BONVILSTON   *St Mary*   ST 064741

The west tower is probably of c1400 with belfry windows of about a century later. The chancel arch is also late medieval but except for the featureless nave north wall most of the nave and chancel date from the restoration of 1863-4 by Pritchard and Seddon. The font carved with leaves is of c1200 and there is a pillar piscina in the chancel. The crudely carved figure under a round arch on the nave west wall is of uncertain date but may be Norman. There is a tablet to Christopher Bassett, d1764.

Bonvilston Church

BRIDGEND   *St Mary*   SS 905795

John Pritchard's fine church of 1885-7 in Merthyr Mawr Road, Nolton, contains a small octagonal font said to be of 1632. For St Illtyd's see Newcastle Bridgend.

BRITON FERRY   *St Mary*   SS 736943

At the west end of the short south aisle of the large church of 1891 with timber arcade piers is a small 16th century tower. The only other ancient features are the tub font and a 17th century window reset at the west end.

CADOXTON-JUXTA-BARRY   *St Cadoc*   ST 130693

One early round-headed window was reset in the north wall of the nave, which was otherwise totally rebuilt in 1885. Another early window is reset on the south side of the 15th century saddle-back roofed west tower with a moulded doorway built at the expense of the Andrews family of Cadoxton Court. Also 15th century are the vaulted south porch, the rood staircase in the SE corner, and most of the chancel with a wagon roof with parts of a former embattled wagon roof and one two-light south window. The east window is of 1828 and the north wall (which is not flush with the nave wall like on the south) probably retains early masonry under the whitewash. The stoup and font with roll mouldings at top and bottom are medieval, and there are 17th century altar rails enclosing the altar on three sides.

Briton Ferry Church

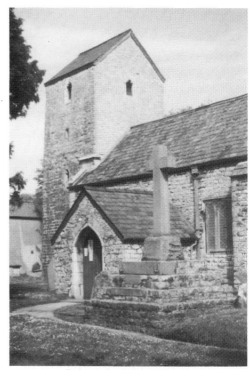

Cadoxton-juxta-Barry Church

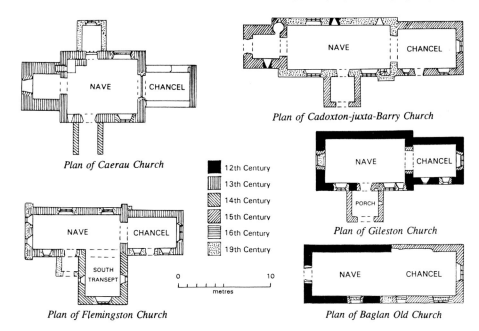

Plan of Caerau Church

Plan of Cadoxton-juxta-Barry Church

12th Century
13th Century
14th Century
15th Century
16th Century
19th Century

Plan of Gileston Church

Plan of Flemingston Church

Plan of Baglan Old Church

CADOXTON-JUXTA-NEATH   *St Catwg*   SS 756986

Most of the church has been rebuilt, a north aisle having been added in 1843, a new east window with stained glass inserted in 1860, and the other windows, chancel arch and probably also the north arcade replaced in 1871. The chief relic of the church built by Adam, Abbot of Neath in the late 13th century is the west tower with keeled rolls on the west doorway arch. A mid 18th century tablet commemorates members of the Llewelyn family of Ynysgerwn and probably of about the same period is the heraldic panel of polychrome lead showing their arms.

CAERAU   *St Mary*   ST 135750

Beside a ringwork overlooking one of Cardiff's western suburbs are ruins of a 13th century church with a tiny chancel (now reduced to footings), an almost square nave, and a west tower which had a saddle-back roof and a west doorway, now blocked. The porch had a tunnel vault. The church remained intact until the early 1970s.

CAERPHILLY   *St Martin*   ST 156865

A medieval font with an octagonal bowl keeled down to a square base survives in the large church, the oldest part of which is of 1877-9. The nave was lengthened in 1904, a NW tower was added in 1907-10, and the south aisle was widened in 1938.

CAPEL LLANILLTERN   *St Ellteyrn*   ST 095799

G.E.Street rebuilt this chapel-of-ease to St Fagans for the Windsor family in 1862 but it still contains a 13th century font with leaves on the bowl, an inscribed 5th or 6th century Early Christian grave slab in the north wall, and several monuments, the earliest being to John Williams, d1651, and Morgan Williams, d1763.

CARDIFF   *St John the Baptist*   ST 183764

St John's was originally a chapel-of-ease to St Mary's (see page 73). The arcade between the chancel and south chapel probably goes back to c1300 but the building was otherwise rebuilt during the second half of the 15th century, one of its patrons being Anne Neville, wife of the Duke of Gloucester, later Richard III. It then had a nave and aisles with arcades of five bays with lozenge-shaped piers, a spectacular diagonally-buttressed west tower of the Somerset type with the lowest stage forming a vaulted open porch with arches or doorways on all four sides, and a chancel with north and south chapels of two bays and a clerestory. The windows were renewed in 1852, and then in 1889-91 those in the aisles were reset when outer aisles were added to replace the galleries of 1813. The south outer aisle is particularly wide and now has its western half mostly filled with vestries and offices. A vestry has also been added east of the south chapel of the chancel. Thus the only medieval work externally is the western bay of the north aisle and the tower. The west tower was probably begun shortly after Anne Neville's death in 1484. It has a five-light west window with a transom and panel tracery. The upper windows are of two lights. The summit has a crown with pierced parapets with raised centres and octagonal corner turrets like cages with miniature pinnacles surrounding their central pinnacles. Each corner of the main tower has a gargoyle from which rises a pinnacle connected by flyers to the corner turrets. Most of the furnishings and monuments are 19th century but the Herbert chapel on the north side of the chancel has screens containing 16th century work, and it contains effigies of two of the family, Sir William, d1609, and the lawyer Sir John, d1617.

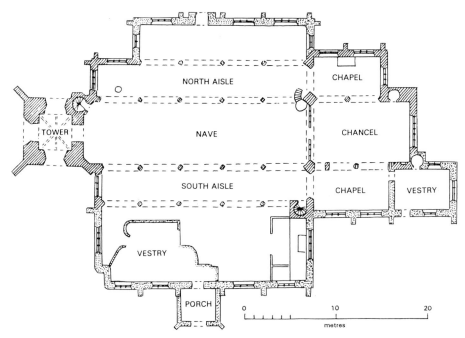

Plan of St John's Church at Cardiff

St John's Church, Cardiff

St John's Church, Cardiff

CARDIFF *St Mary* ST 182803

The original parish church of Cardiff was St Mary's, which also served a priory which was a daughter house of Tewkesbury Abbey. A parochial aisle was added in 1221 and other additions made later. In the early 17th century Speed depicted it as a cruciform building with a central tower, but it was then under threat of undermining by the River Taff, and was abandoned two generations later. There are no remains and the present church of St Mary of 1840 lies on a different site.

CILYBEBYLL *St John the Evangelist* SN 744047

The short west tower with a corbelled parapet may be late 16th century. The nave and chancel are thought to be mostly of a rebuilding in 1868, although two windows could represent an earlier campaign of remodelling in 1837. There is a tablet to Richard Herbert, d1725, and outside is the base of a medieval churchyard cross.

Coity Church

COITY   *St Mary*   SS 924815

This 14th century cruciform church has a wagon-roofed nave which is much wider than the transepts and chancel. The triple sedilia in the blue-painted chancel, three 14th century effigies of members of the Turberville family, the south doorway with its porch, the priest's doorway, and the windows, including one at the west end of five lights with intersecting tracery with pointed trefoils, all survived the restoration of 1860. The transepts have squints towards the chancel and the north transept also has an opening from the nave. The crossing piers and vault are also original, although the tower top, reached by a curious corbelled stair in the north transept, is 16th century, and has a corbelled parapet. Parts of the much restored wooden Easter Sepulchre with panels showing emblems of the Passion date from c1500.

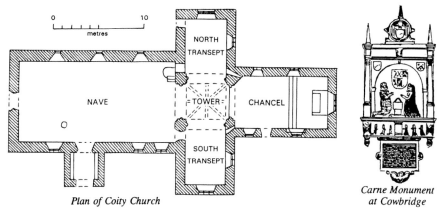

Plan of Coity Church

*Carne Monument
at Cowbridge*

COLWINSTON   *St Michael*   SS 939755

A pair of 14th century ogival-headed image niches with traces of wall-painting, flank the plain Norman chancel arch. One niche contains a figure of a bishop, thought to represent St Nicholas of Myra. The chancel has a pair of 13th century lancets rebated for external shutters on the south, a moulded 14th century tomb-recess arch in the north wall now containing a later medieval effigy, and a two-light 15th century east window. The south porch and embattled west tower with a three-light window over the west doorway are 16th century. There is a tablet to David Thomas, d1769.

COWBRIDGE   *Holy Cross*   SS 994746

As built in the late 13th century to serve the newly-founded town as a chapel-of-ease to Llanblethian, the church comprised a spacious nave, a central tower and a chancel. The tower has a north lancet and broaches to an embattled top which is said to have once had a spire, and the chancel has an original piscina of Sutton stone. Traces of other north lancets can be seen on either side of the large 16th century window west of the Victorian north porch. The expense of adding the two bay north chapel and the Llanquian aisle along the south side of the nave and tower is said to have been borne by the Lady Anne Neville in the 1470s. The wide windows of this period in the nave, aisle and chapel were renewed during John Pritchard's restoration of 1850-2 and the five bay arcade with four-centred arches upon piers with four shafts and four hollows was rebuilt using the original material in 1926. In the 16th century a vestry was added beyond the east wall at the junction of chapel and chancel. The octagonal font is probably 14th century. The monuments include one with kneeling effigies of William Carne of Nash Manor, d1616 and his wife and family, and a tablet to Richard Jenkins, d1721.

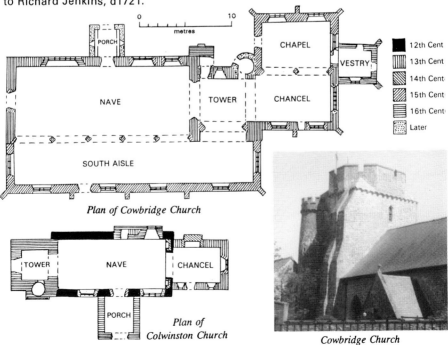

0   10
metres

PORCH

CHAPEL

VESTRY

NAVE

TOWER

CHANCEL

■ 12th Cent

▥ 13th Cent

▨ 14th Cent

▧ 15th Cent

▤ 16th Cent

▦ Later

SOUTH AISLE

Plan of Cowbridge Church

TOWER

NAVE

CHANCEL

PORCH

Plan of Colwinston Church

Cowbridge Church

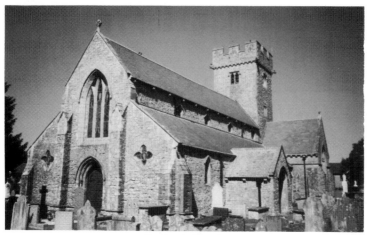

Coychurch Church

COYCHURCH   *St Crallo*   SS 939797

Being larger than most of the surrounding medieval churches, this cruciform building of c1270-1300 is sometimes called "The Cathedral of the Vale". It has a long but comparatively narrow nave and aisles with arcades of four bays with octagonal piers. The west wall has a fine shafted doorway below a three-light window whilst the aisles have rare quatrefoil-shaped end windows. There is a clerestory of cinquefoil shaped windows on the south side only. The south transept had to be rebuilt after it was destroyed by the collapse of the original central tower in 1877, and the chancel with close-set trefoil-headed lancets linked internally by a hoodmould, and a three-light east window with intersecting tracery is also somewhat restored. The tower has a NW stair turret supported on a section of solid walling instead of a fifth arcade arch. The nave has a 15th century font and a wagon roof of that period with angels holding shields and foliage bosses. Now brought inside the church are fragments of two 10th or 11th century churchyard crosses. In the north transept are a recumbent effigy of a 14th century priest, a recumbent effigy of vicar Thomas Ivans, d1591, and an 18th century tablet to the Thomas family.

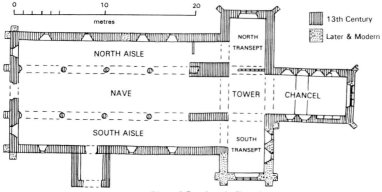

Plan of Coychurch Church

CRYNANT   *St Margaret*   SN 795048

South of the church of 1909 is the small original chapel-of-ease, said to be medieval, although the pointed-arched windows with wooden Y-tracery are of c1800.

CWMAVON   *St Michael*   SN 780920

The nave, north aisle, south porch and chancel are all of 1850-1 by John Pritchard. Older relics are the west tower of 1660 with a spire and yellow brick battlements probably of about a century later, the tub font and the late 16th century tomb chest with effigies of twelve children which now forms part of the altar.

EGLWYS BREVIS   *St Brevis*   ST 006691

Within the airbase is a small 13th century nave and chancel church with cusped east lancets, a pillar piscina. and a tiny embattled bellcote corbelled out from both the east and west sides of the west wall. The south porch and the windows either side of it are 16th century. There are 17th century texts on the interior walls and royal arms of William and Mary. The Norman tub font has a rope moulding round the top.

EGLWYSILAN   *St Ilan*   ST 106890

The church lies high up, and alone except for an inn. The spacious nave probably has 13th century walling but the roof and windows are of 1873, except for one of three arched lights, probably 18th century, on the south side. On the north wall is a slab carved with a crude outline of an 8th, 9th or 10th century warrior. The font is also old. The comparatively small chancel has no features of interest but there is an embattled west tower with short corner pinnacles, perhaps of the 16th century.

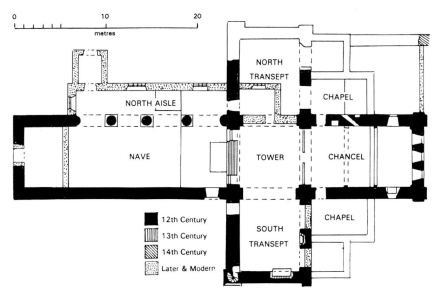

Plan of Ewenny Priory Church

EWENNY   *St Michael*   SS 912778

A church founded here c1120 by William de Londres was consecrated by Urban, Bishop of Llandaff. The building is clearly monastic in plan (see p77), being cruciform, with two ruined chapels east of each transept, the inner chapels being longer, yet the Benedictine priory with monks from St Peter's Abbey at Gloucester only seems to have been established by William's son Maurice in 1141. Either the eastern parts are later or the church of c1120 was always intended for a priory. Its nave, now shorn of its west bay since c1800, and the north aisle with a four bay arcade of circular piers with clerestory windows above them, served the parishioners, as they do now. The aisle has 16th century windows and a porch of that period, although they were rebuilt in 1895. The nave has a SE doorway towards the former cloister.

The chancel with triple east windows and the tower and south transept were divided off at the Reformation and are now in the custody of Cadw, whilst the north transept is badly ruined. A 19th century vestry adjoins the 16th century wall closing of the north arch of the crossing. The western arch is also walled off, which the east arch contains a screen, the upper part of which is 14th century, although the linenfold panels below are early 16th century. The tower originally rose only slightly above the former steeply-pitched roofs of the adjoining arms, but c1300, when the precinct was enclosed with a fortified wall (see the companion volume The Castles of Gwent, Glamorgan and Gower), the tower was given a new embattled top with arrowloops. Its upper stage is reached by means of a passage in the south transept west wall from a spiral stair in the SW corner. The chancel has a barrel vault with ribs supported on pilasters corbelled out above a plain dado, and the crossing has the same pattern, the arches being supported on short pairs of columns above the dado.

There are several 10th to 12th century gravestones and four early 13th century cross-slabs for Maurice de Londres and (probably) his son William, d1205, and his grandson, another William, who died shortly afterwards, and one of the priors of that period. There is also a slab incised with a female figure to Hawise de Londres, d1274, and an effigy of a cross-legged knight. There are monuments to some of the Carnes, who created a house out of the cloistral buildings, including a tomb chest to Edward, d1650, upon which is an inscription to John, d1700, and there is a tablet to Richard, d1713, and there is also a tablet to Richard Turbeville, d1771. See plan on page 77.

Gileston Church

FLEMINGSTON   *St Michael*   ST 016701

The church was heavily restored in 1858 but originally the nave and chancel were 13th century, the period of the font with a square bowl on a round stem. The roofs are 15th century and the south transept with an end window with cusped intersecting tracery was added in the early 14th century, no doubt at the expense of Joan le Fleming, whose effigy (now reversed) lies under the arch towards the nave.

GELLIGAER   *St Catwg*   ST 136969

The shapes of the south doorways of the spacious nave and chancel suggest that they are both 13th century, and the west tower and porch are early 16th century, but the north buttresses, all the windows except one on the north and the total immersion font by the entrance are of Charles Buckeridge's restoration of 1867.

GILESTON   *St Giles*   ST 017671

The tub font looks Norman, and possibly also a chancel south window. The church seems to have been mostly rebuilt during the late 15th century and has of that period a porch, the east window, the screen, the very heavily restored roofs, and a door with the arms of the patrons. The south windows of both nave and chancel, however, could be 14th century. There are several monuments to the Giles family, especially that of William, d1724, and there is also a tablet to Ann Willis, d1760.

GLYNCORRWG   *St John the Baptist*   SN 874994

The existing church is of 1905 by Bruce Vaughan, and only the font and a few tablets predate the opening up of this once remote valley in the 1850s.

HIGHLIGHT   ST 707698

Footings remain of a nave and chancel church abandoned by the 17th century.

Arch at Ewenny Priory   *Tower of Ewenny Priory*

Laleston Church

LALESTON   *St David*   SS 875799

The nave masonry may be 13th century but the chancel arch looks 14th century. Of the 15th century are the south doorway and wagon-roofed porch with ogee-headed doorways, the roodloft staircase, and the west tower with a vaulted lowest stage, gargoyles at the summit, and the unusual arrangement of a pair of two-light belfry windows facing west. The nave and chancel windows are of 1871. There is a tablet to Thomas Bennet, d1772, and there are several slightly earlier tablets.

LAVERNOCK   *St Lawrence*   ST 187682

The windowless north wall of this tiny nave and chancel church above the cliffs betray its medieval origin, although the openings and roofs are now all of 1852.

LISVANE   *St Denys*   ST 192831

The flattened double-chamfered arches from the nave towards the chancel and north transept suggest an early 14th century date for all three parts, although the windows are all 19th century. The west tower with a saddleback roof on a corbel table could be late 14th century. The only old furnishing is an octagonal font. Work carried out in 1979 included extending the transept, new furnishings and adding a church hall.

LLANBAD   *St Peter*   SS 993853

Regular services at this remotely located church ended in 1812 and it has since been reduced to the lower parts of the walls of a 13th or 14th century nave with a later medieval chancel and south porch. The existing west end is still later. Excavations revealed traces of two early churches thought to have been destroyed in the 6th and 8th centuries respectively, plus memorial stones, one of which mentions a 6th century king thought to be the warrior upon which the legend of King Arthur is based.

Lisvane Church

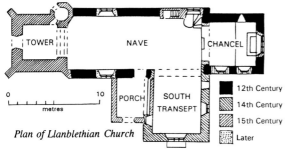

Plan of Llanblethian Church

■	12th Century
▨	14th Century
▨	15th Century
▦	Later

LLANBLETHIAN *St John Baptist* SS 985740

The low chancel has a Norman window on the north side and the nave and tub-shaped font may also be of that date, although the dating of the south doorway is uncertain. It lies off centre to the ashlar-faced 15th century porch which adjoins a 14th century south transept. The transept contains a tomb recess in which is an effigy of a 13th century civilian found under the tower, and it lies over a vaulted crypt discovered in 1896, when 200 skeletons were found within it. The chancel has trefoil-headed lancets on the south and a 15th century east window. The fine diagonally-buttressed west tower with a polygonal stair turret at the NE corner is said to have been built in the 1470s with Anne Neville as patron. Pinnacles rise from the tops of the buttresses and there are gargoyles. Also 15th century are the staircase to the former rood loft and perhaps parts of the roof. There is also a tablet of 1763 to Sir Leoline Jenkins, a late 17th century Principal of Jesus College, Oxford.

Llanblethian Church

LLANCARFAN   *St Cadoc*   ST 052703

The Norman-looking window high up on the south side of the tower is probably of 1877 and the tower arch suggests the 13th century as a more likely date. The nave and chancel are probably of the 1190s, the plain pointed arch between them being set on imposts with crude carvings of Xs in squares. The south arcade of double-chamfered steeply pointed arcades on square piers with the abaci corbelled out on heads and bunches of grapes is 13th century. The south doorway of that period with shafts and roll-mouldings on the arch was reset in the early 14th century when the aisle was widened and extended as far as the chancel east wall, which dates from the same period. The aisle has two light windows with Y-tracery, and the chapel in its eastern end has a three bay arcade towards the chancel and a three light window with intersecting tracery. Of the 15th century are the porch, the windows in the aisle west wall and nave north wall, the huge square-headed five-light window in the chancel north wall, a damaged reredos and the chapel screen. Painted on the nave south wall is a 17th century Apostles' Creed. The nine-sided font with leaves underneath is 14th century and there is a stoup beside the south doorway.

LLANDOUGH   *St Dochwy*   SS 996729

The chancel and chancel arch were rebuilt in 1869 by Charles Buckeridge, who added a north vestry, but there is a brass of Wenllian Walshe, d1427, and of about the same period are the west window set high up, the roodloft staircase and the small windows which lighted the screen, plus south porch with its original roof with leaf-bosses and a central head of Christ. There is also a medieval octagonal font.

LLANDOUGH   *St Dochwy*   ST 168733

The church itself was entirely rebuilt in 1865 by S.C.Fripp but there is a replica of a Norman arch with chevrons from its predecessor and in the churchyard lies the 3m high Irbic Cross, a Celtic relic complete except for the cross-head. It has much interlace carving and figures including clerics on the tapering base.

Llandough Church   *Brass at Llandough*

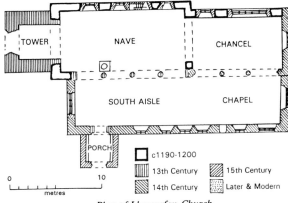

Plan of Llancarfan Church

Llancarfan Church

LLANDOW   *Holy Trinity*   SS 943734

The round-headed south doorway, the tub font, and the slightly pointed chancel arch on simple imposts may all be Norman. The segmental-arched niches flanking the chancel arch and the partly rebuilt blind arch framing all three openings may be later. The small saddleback-roofed west tower with trefoiled belfry lancets is 13th century, and the chancel also has one lancet. The priest's doorway, south porch, and one south window are 15th century.

LLANDYFODWG   *St Tyfodwg*   SS 956872

The early 16th century tower of this dramatically positioned church has a corbelled parapet and paired arched lights for belfry openings. The nave was restored from a very decayed condition in the 1870s by Pritchard and the chancel was entirely rebuilt in 1893, although the doorway to the roodloft staircase is late medieval, as is the octagonal font. On the floor by the altar is a shallow relief effigy of a medieval pilgrim. There is also a tablet to George Lucas, d1688.

LLANEDEYRN   *St Edeyrn*   ST 221820

Each side of the nave has a small Norman window and a large three-light window of c1500. Of the latter period are the loft staircase and the west tower with its west doorway with a four-centred head. The vaulted south porch may be 14th century. The chancel is the same width as the nave and has a canopied medieval image niche reset in its east wall rebuilt in 1888, when the chancel arch was probably widened.

LLANFRYNACH   *St Brynach*   SS 979747

The chancel has a trefoil-headed 13th century piscina and is divided from the nave by a plain pointed arch on simple imposts. One chancel window looks 16th century and two others, including the east window, are blocked. The south doorway with hollow chamfers could be either 14th or 15th century. The late 15th century tower has a SE stair turret and a corbelled parapet. One south window is 19th century and one with wooden mullions on the north side is of 1968, but otherwise the church has seen little restoration. It has a late medieval roof, traces of wall paintings beside the chancel arch and a font dated 1745.

LLANGAN   *St Canna*   SS 957778

The church itself was mostly rebuilt in 1856 and the only ancient structural feature is the doorway to the roodloft staircase. The tub font with semi-circles underneath may be 13th century, there are fragments of an 11th century cross-head in the porch, and fragments of tombstones of the same period are set into the chancel east and south walls. There is also a tablet to John Thomas, d1764. West of the church lies a 9th or 10th century wheel cross-head showing the Crucifixion. In front of the church lies a complete 15th century churchyard cross with the head having saints on the north and south sides, a Pieta on the east and the Crucifixion on the west.

LLANGEINOR   *St Cein*   SS 924879

The church lies on a high ridge with only an inn for company. Halliday's restoration of 1894 has left only a tub font and some evidence of the former screen and loft as the only old features of the nave and chancel. There is a late medieval west tower with a corbelled parapet and pairs of arched belfry lights under hoodmoulds.

LLANGIWG   *St Ciwg*   SN 724057

The windowless north wall remains medieval, but the rebuilding of 1812 recorded on a tablet on the south wall seems to have involved the removal of the chancel arch and the corbelled parapets of the tower as well as the insertion of windows with Y-tracery. There is an early tub-shaped font.

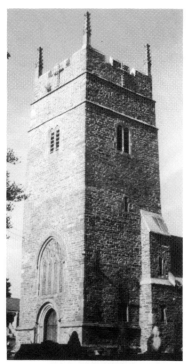

Llangynwyn Church

LLANGYNWYD   *St Cennydd*   SS 857889

On the porch outer arch are the initials of Olive Talbot of Margam, for whom the nave and chancel were mostly rebuilt in 1891-3, although the windowless medieval north wall still remains, along with an octagonal 14th century font and the 13th century roll-moulded priest's doorway and one lancet of the chancel, which also has one 14th century window. The 15th century west tower is unusual for this district, having a large window over a wide doorway set into a moulded plinth, and a vault and high tower arch, in one side of which is a doorway to the stair in the SE corner. The top is set back twice above the cinquefoiled twin bell-openings, and has battlements with corner pinnacles. There is a tablet to Hopkin Hopkin, d1742.

LLANHARRY   *St Illtyd*   ST 006805

The church was rebuilt in 1868 by David Vaughan but retains an octagonal font with simple shapes on the faces and a comparatively narrow chancel arch, both probably 15th century. There is also a cast iron memorial slab to William Gibbon, d1759.

LLANILID *St Illid and St Curig* SS 977813

The unusual step-headed east window probably of the early 17th century is the chief feature of interest. The tower is dated 1636 but has bell-openings which are 16th century, as are the south doorways, porch and several south windows, but the plain narrow pointed tower arch and chancel arch could be 13th century, the likely age of the tub font with linked trefoils in shallow relief. The church was restored in 1882.

LLANILLTUD FAERDREF *St Illtyd* ST 082866

The small saddleback-roofed west tower is dated 1636 over the west doorway but is probably older. The nave and chancel are said to have been rebuilt in the 1520s and of that period are one renewed north window in the chancel and a three-light south window now looking into the extensions of the 1970s providing a south aisle and vestries. The north windows with Y-tracery probably date from 1874.

LLANISHEN *St Isan* ST 176818

The 13th century chancel has one original lancet, a piscina with a shelf, a 15th century east window with diamond-shaped hoodmould stops, and 14th century windows on either side of the sanctuary. The nave has an original south porch and over the small inner doorway is a 15th relief of the Crucifixion flanked by saints. The west tower has corbelled battlements and 15th century two-light belfry openings. These parts now form the south aisle of a fully aisled church of 1907-8, replacing a north aisle added in 1854, the arcade of which survives. In the old chancel is a brass to Matthew Pritchard, d1623, and there is a tablet to Thomas Lewis, 1764.

Llanishen Church

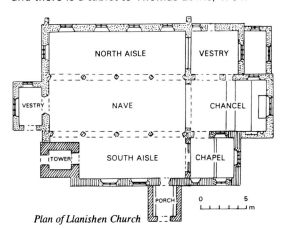

Plan of Llanishen Church

East window at Llanilid

LLANMAES   *St Catwg*   SS 981694

The lofty west tower bears the date 1632 and the south windows of the nave could also be that late, whilst one north window is of 1882. The chancel has renewed 13th century lancets on the south, and the jambs, at least, of the chancel arch are of that period. A 15th century screen remains, plus the access stair to its former loft. The font is Norman and there is part of a wall painting of St George and the Dragon.

LLANMIHANGEL   *St Michael*   SS 982719

The round chancel arch suggests a Norman origin for the nave and chancel. The trefoiled lancet with a rebate for a shutter on the north side is probably 14th century. In the restoration of 1888 the porch was added and a two-light 16th century window was moved from the east wall to the north side to allow the insertion of a larger window. At that time a stair turret was added on the north side of the 15th century tower and a crossloop reset in it. The tower has two other crossloops and a saddleback roof corbelled on all four sides. There is an old font. There are 18th century tablets to Sir Humphrey Edwin and his family and Charles Edwin, and a recumbent half effigy of Griffith Grant, d1591, holding a heart.

Llantrisant Church

LLANQUIAN   *St James*   ST 018744

An outbuilding of a farm on Stalling Down is a much altered medieval chapel-of-ease to Cowbridge with the unusual feature of an attached priest's house at the west end.

LLANSANNOR   *St Senwyr*   SS 994775

The chancel was rebuilt as wide as the nave in the late 13th century, the east window with trefoil-headed lights and priest's doorway being of that date. The south porch and the tiny west tower with a four-gabled roof are 16th century. The roodloft stair, nave roof, and a west doorway now looking into the tower are 15th century. The chancel arch was widened in the 19th century, when new windows were provided on the south side. The octagonal font may be 14th century. There is a fragment of a wall-painting of St Christopher on the south wall. There are tablets to the Truman family and Edward Eustace, d1708, and an effigy of a crosslegged knight of c1400, probably Gronw Ab Ifor.

Llansannor Church

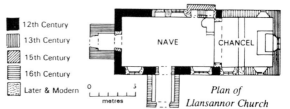

■ 12th Century
▥ 13th Century
▨ 15th Century
☰ 16th Century
▦ Later & Modern

NAVE   CHANCEL

0   5
metres

*Plan of
Llansannor Church*

Llantrisant Church

LLANTRISANT   *St Illtyd, St Wonno and St Dyfodwg*   ST 046834

Until John Pritchard's restoration of 1872-4 there were Norman five-bay arcades dividing the nave and aisles of this large hilltop church. The outer walls may be 15th century, but the south porch is 17th century and the north porch and buttresses are of 1872, whilst the chancel could be of any date. The late 15th century tower of two stages is diagonally buttressed, with a moulded plinth and a polygonal NE stair turret, and has a west doorway of 1894, when an immersion font was formed in its base. There is also a 15th century octagonal font with stars in circles. The 18th century chandelier was made in Bristol. The monuments include a worn effigy of one of the 13th century Welsh lords of Meisgyn, and a mid-18th century tablet to Dr Richard Thomas and a number of others.

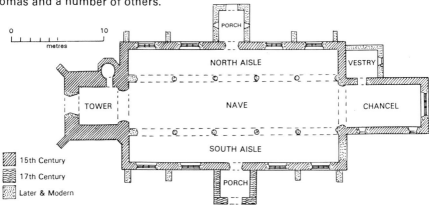

Plan of Llantrisant Church

Chancel arch, Llantwit Major

LLANTRITHYD   *St Illtyd*

ST 043727

The chancel arch and the south doorway and one window in the nave are early 14th century. The north walls have been refaced externally. The chancel was rebuilt in 1656, the year that appears over the step-headed east window. The 16th century west tower has a top stage rebuilt in 1711. Near it, outside, is a Norman arcaded bowl, either a font or a cross-base. The font inside the church is mid 17th century and has a cartouche on each face. Other cartouches on alabaster of the same century have come from the adjacent house. The painted screen is 15th century. There are said to be several incised slabs under the chancel carpet. Other monuments include a small effigy of a 14th century civilian, a tomb of 1597 with effigies of Sir Anthony Mansell, his wife Elizabeth Basset, their children and her parents, and wall-monuments of Sir John Aubrey, d1700, and Sir Thomas Aubrey and his wife, 1788.

Llantwit Major Church

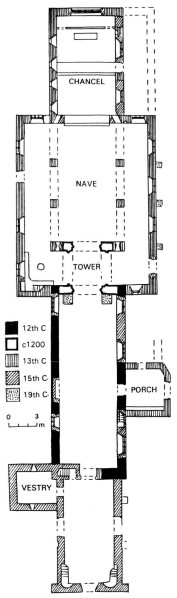

Plan of Llantwit Major Church

LLANTWIT MAJOR   St Illtyd   SS 966687

The school founded here c500 by St Illtyd lasted until the 12th century, the period of the font carved with scales and the round arched south doorway. A central tower set on clustered piers with keeled shafts and transepts were built at the east end c1200. The transepts lost their separate gables and the crossing arches and tower above were rebuilt in the late 13th century when, to serve a college of canons, these parts were incorporated into the west end of a new aisled nave of three further bays of plain arches on square piers with a chancel and a south chapel. The original nave remained in use to serve the parish and was then given a large new south porch and a new west doorway, now opening towards the ruined 15th century Raglan family chapel. The western corners of the chapel have remains of stairs towards a former gallery at that end. The parish nave has one fine square-headed three-light 14th century window on the south side, an arched-braced roof and other windows of the late 15th century, when a two storey north vestry was added overlapping the junction of the nave and west chapel. About the same time a chapel east of the porch and also the collegiate south chapel were demolished and the two bay arcade between the latter and the chancel was walled up. The chapel south doorway was then reset in the blocking of one of the arches. The aisles have squints towards the chancel and the north aisle retains original windows, including one with plate-tracery. The chancel also has late 13th century north windows, although the east window was moved in 1905 to the south aisle east wall and replaced by a wider window.

The niche with a figure of Jesse and the heads of his descendants amongst foliage at the east end of the south arcade may have formed part of an early 13th century reredos. The chancel has a late 14th century piscina and integral reredos, behind which was a very narrow vestry space. The various relics of wall painting include a background to a rood over the chancel arch, 13th century figures of the Virgin Mary and Mary Magdalene on the chancel north wall, a 15th century figure of St Christopher on the nave north wall, and royal arms of James I dated 1604.

The parochial nave contains a foliated cross-slab with a priest's head, recumbent effigies of a 14th century priest and an Elizabethan woman, and a tablet to James Seys, d1747. Here also are gathered a number of 9th and 10th century cross fragments. One fine disc-headed cross-shaft similar to one of 839 at Tullylease, Co Cork, has an inscription which appears to refer to Hywell, King of Glywysing, d886 and his father Rhys, and another stone bears the name Samson. In the graveyard are a cross base and a ruined chantry priest's house.

LLANWENSAN   *St Wensan*   ST 081006

A house has been formed out of a chapel with a Norman doorway tympanum in situ.

LLANWONNO   *St Gwynno*   ST 030956

The church lies high up amongst forested hills above the Rhondda and Cynon valleys. The nave and chancel may be 14th century, the likely date of the south doorway and font, and the porch is medieval, despite the renewed outer doorway. The west porch supporting a saddleback-roofed belfry and the south windows are of 1893, and the larger north windows are of 1913. Reset in the south wall are fragments of two cross-slabs probably going back to the 9th century.

LLYSWORNEY   *St Tydfil*   SS 962741

The plain central tower has pointed arches offset to the north towards both nave and chancel. The layout suggests that originally there was a narrower Norman nave (similar in width to the chancel), from which has probably come the crudely carved ornamental stone now set upon the SE corner of the existing nave. The tower has a corbelled parapet and belfry windows of c1500. The squint beside the chancel arch and the windows are of the restoration of 1893-4 by Bruton and Williams, but the north vestry and south porch are probably older. There is an old octagonal font and there are late 17th century altar rails with turned balusters. See page 8.

MARCROSS   *Holy Trinity*   SS 922692

The Norman nave and chancel have a chancel arch with a roll-moulding and chevrons and a south doorway with shafts with foliage capitals and a millet-moulded arch with grotesque heads. The font with top and bottom rolls also looks Norman. The chancel has trefoil-headed lancets rebated externally for shutters. There is also a saddleback-roofed west tower. The tomb recess in the nave north wall is 14th century.

Marcross Church

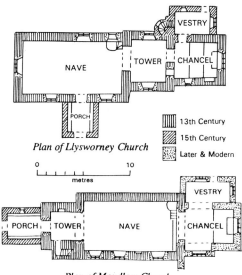

Plan of Llysworney Church

|||| 13th Century
▨ 15th Century
▦ Later & Modern

0   10
metres

Plan of Maudlam Church

MARGAM *St Mary* SS 802864 & 802866

Six bays of the eight bay aisled nave of the Cistercian abbey church founded in 1147 survive in use as the parish church. Only the centre of the west front and the six bay arcades of round arches of two orders on elongated cruciform piers survived the rebuilding of 1805-10 for Thomas Mansel Talbot, when the clerestory windows immediately above the arches were blocked up. Parts of the outer walls of the choir aisles, south transept chapels, and circular chapter house, all of c1200-20, also remain in the grounds of the ruined 19th century mansion. There are no old furnishings but the many Mansel monuments include three tombs with effigies of Sir Rice, d1559, Sir Edward, d1585, and Sir Thomas, d1631, with their wives, plus effigies of Sir Lewis, d1638, and a tablet to Thomas, 1705. There are also kneeling effigies of Raleigh Bussy, d1623, and his wife, and Katherine Bussy, d1625.

West doorway at Margam

   The early 19th century schoolroom NW of the church now houses a fine collection of Early Christian crosses and fragments dating from the 6th to the 11th centuries, proof that Margam was a major monastic settlement before the coming of the Cistercians, several of whose tomb stones also lie in the museum.

   High above the north side of the abbey, on the shoulder of Craig Fawr is a ruined chapel with a west window of c1300 with a quatrefoil over two trefoiled lights. The east window had 15th century tracery but the mullions are missing. One south window is trefoil-headed. The other openings are defaced.

MAWDLAM *St Mary* SS 806820

The Norman font may have come from the former church at Kenfig to the NW. The nave with a plain north wall is probably 13th century and the tower with a saddleback roof interrupting circulation of the corbelled parapets on the north and south sides is perhaps of the end of that century. West of it is a 15th century porch. The nave south windows are of 1878 and the chancel and chancel arch were rebuilt in 1894, when an organ-chamber was added.

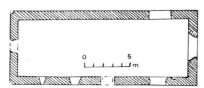

Plan of chapel at Margam

Margam Abbey Church

Merthyr Dyfan Church   *Michaelston-le-Pit Church*

MERTHYR DYFAN   *St Dyfan*   ST 115694

The nave and chancel are 13th century, with one original lancet on the south side. Other windows with foil-headed lights are 15th century, although some are of the restoration of 1857, whilst the tower with a four-centred tower arch and the similar chancel arch may be as late as the 16th century. The floors were lowered during a refurbishment of 1972. The only older furnishing is the tub font. The south doorway and porch are 19th century although the stoup appears to be a reset medieval mortar.

MERTHYR MAWR   *St Teilo*   SS 883776 & 889791

The church itself was entirely rebuilt in 1849-51 to a design by Ferrey, but a quatrefoil-shaped medieval stoup lies by the font, two very damaged medieval effigies lie in the churchyard, and under a shelter north of the church is a collection of 11th and 12th century crosses and gravestones, together with a 5th century stone with an inscription in Roman capitals. On a wooded rock in the private grounds of Merthyr Mawr House is a tiny ruined 15th century oratory with an original doorway, bellcote and two windows. It contains two very fine 11th century cross-shafts with interlace and inscriptions. One was a tombstone, the other recorded a transfer of land.

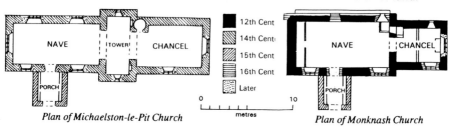

■	12th Cent
▧	14th Cent
▨	15th Cent
▤	16th Cent
▦	Later

0   10
metres

Plan of Michaelston-le-Pit Church   *Plan of Monknash Church*

MERTHYR TYDFIL   *St Tydfil*   SO 049058

A classical style nave of 1820 on the site of the medieval church (supposedly on the site of St Tydfil's martyrdom) was remodelled in the neo-Norman style by Pearson in the 1890s. It contains an 8th or 9th century sone inscribed with the name Artbeu.

MICHAELSTON-LE-PIT   *St Michael*   ST 152730

This church has a saddleback-roofed central tower set over crude crossing arches with transepts that are no more than deep recesses for altars, one having a squint and the other an aumbry. The south doorway with a stoup beside it and the font may be 14th century and the whole building is probably of that period, but with a porch and one window of the 15th century and other windows of the 19th century. There are old pews and an 18th century three-decker pulpit, the only one in the Vale.

MICHAELSTON-SUPER-ELY   *St Michael*   ST 115763

The course of herringbone masonry low down on the north wall dates the church as Norman, but the chancel arch of that period was replaced during the restoration of 1863 by David Vaughan. The south doorway, the octagonal font, and one cusped and ogival-headed lancet are 14th century and there are also two restored 15th century windows, one of which was moved from the east wall in 1863 to make way for a larger window there. The tiny chapel in the nave SE corner (hardly big enough to call a transept), the porch and the saddleback-roofed west tower have all been rebuilt. The blocked arch in the chancel north wall was for a vestry proposed in 1908 but never completed. The heraldic tablet dated 1546 commemorates a land transfer.

MONKNASH   *St Mary*   SS 921705

The narrow round chancel arch and the small roll-moulded NE window show that the nave and chancel are Norman. The nave north wall has been rebuilt with a substantial battered base. The south doorway and windows of two and three light with hoodmoulds are 16th century, although the arch-braced roof, south porch and octagonal font may be slightly earlier. The east window is of 1860.

NEATH   *St Thomas*   SS 754977

The late 15th century diagonally buttressed west tower with a moulded plinth is all that remains of the medieval building. The aisled nave with arcades of round arches on square piers and the chancel with a Venetian east window are both of 1730, with a contemporary font and royal arms. Tracery was inserted in the round-headed windows in 1874. The oldest monument is that of Sir Robert Mackworth, d1794.

Merthyr Mawr Chapel   *Monknash Church*

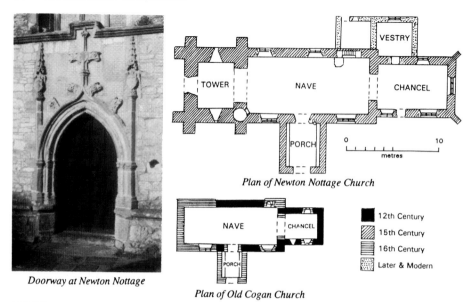

Doorway at Newton Nottage

Plan of Newton Nottage Church

NAVE

CHANCEL

PORCH

■ 12th Century
▨ 15th Century
▤ 16th Century
▦ Later & Modern

Plan of Old Cogan Church

NEATH   *St Illtyd*   SS 763981

This church lies above the river 1km east of the town centre. It has an early round chancel arch and a blocked priest's doorway which looks 13th century, but the nave south wall, porch, north transept and all the windows date from the drastic restoration of 1858. The west tower with a corbelled parapet is older than the west doorway and window of c1500 cut into the batter of the lower walls.

NEWCASTLE BRIDGEND   *St Illtyd*   SS 903801

The church lies in an elevated position beside the castle ruin. The early 16th century west tower has a moulded plinth, a four-centred head to the west doorway, and corbelled battlements with small pinnacles and gargoyles. The nave and south porch were rebuilt by John Pritchard in 1849-50, when a north aisle was added. In 1893-4 Bruce Vaughan rebuilt the chancel and added a north chapel. Most of the furnishings date from then, except for an octagonal font bowl with quatrefoils carved in relief.

NEWTON NOTTAGE   *St John the Baptist*   SS 837775

The nave, chancel, large south porch, the stone pulpit reached by an arch through the wall, and the west tower appear to be all of the late 15th century, although the nave was heavily restored by Pritchard and Seddon in 1860. The tower is unusually large, being as wide as the nave, and has thick walls and massive corner buttresses. The tower arch is wide and tall and has semi-circular responds and the west doorway has a crocketed hoodmould with flanking pinnacles. The tower has a saddleback-roof with corbelled parapets on the north and south sides. On the east side it has corbels for some sort of platform. The chancel has diagonal buttresses, a moulded plinth, windows of two and three lights with renewed tracery and a priest's doorway with decorated spandrels and a hoodmould rising from shield-bearing angels. The only older feature is a 13th century stoup by the south doorway. There are 17th century texts painted on the nave north wall. There is a tablet to Richard Loughor, d1722.

OLD COGAN *St Peter* ST 168706

The tiny nave and chancel both have herringbone masonry of c1100 and are divided by a plain round arch. The chancel has no east window but there are late medieval windows on either side of the sanctuary. The nave was lengthened westward in the 16th century, when it was provided with new south windows and a porch. The church was derelict before the light restoration of 1865 for the Marquis of Bute.

PENDEYERN *St Cynoc* SN 945086

The church itself dates from 1843, repaired and remodelled in 1876 and 1895 but it has 15th century foliage bosses remaining in the chancel roof, a polygonal medieval stoup by the doorway and a small late medieval west tower with a corbelled parapet.

PENDOYLAN *St Cadoc* ST 060767

The large west tower with a corbelled parapet has a west doorway of c1500 with a four-centred arch, but the rough vault and roll-moulded doorway to the staircase suggests the structure may go back two hundred years earlier. The chancel arch and the roodloft stair on the north side are also of c1500. During a heavy restoration of 1855 the whole of the chancel east wall and the south side of the church were rebuilt, and a new porch provided. The font, if medieval, has been recut.

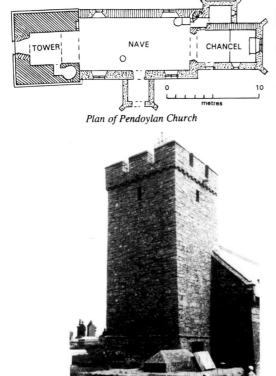

Plan of Pendoylan Church

Penderyn Church　　　　　*Pendoylan Church*

PENMARK   *St Mary*   ST 058689

The pointed chancel arch of c1200 has chevrons on the roll-moulding and heads on the chamfered imposts. The south doorway suggests that the nave is a 14th century rebuilding, and perhaps also the chancel, although its windows are of 1860. In the nave the ceiled wagon roof, two windows, and the roodloft stair projection are 15th century. Also of that date is the embattled west tower with a wide and tall wave-moulded arch towards the nave. The font is 13th century, the altar rails are of c1700, and the pulpit is 18th century. The monuments include those of Catherine Lewis, d1682, and Thomas Lewis, d1689, and Robert and Mary Jones, c1756. See page 9.

PENRHYS   *St Mary*   ST 002945

Penrhys was an important place of pilgrimage in the 16th century, noted for its miracle-working image of the Virgin. Just a short length of the chancel north wall remains beside a bus-stop by a car park on top of a ridge. Close by is a statue of the Virgin erected in 1953, and not far away on the hillside is an old well-chapel.

PENTYRCH   *St Cadwg*   ST 104817

The church was rebuilt in 1853-7 by Pritchard & Seddon. Older features are the font, stoup and foliated cross-slab at the west end.

PETERSTON-SUPER-ELY   *St Peter*   ST 083764

The west tower with its wide and high tower arch and corbelled battlements and gargoyles is 15th century, and the nave also has tall three-light windows and a small octagonal font of that period. The chancel was mostly rebuilt in 1890-1 but the chamfered chancel arch set over plain jambs is 14th century.

PORTHKERRY   *St Curig*   ST 083665

The nave and small chancel with one south lancet are 13th century but the chancel arch is of 1867. The east window, the screen, and the west tower with a corbelled parapet are 15th century, and the square-headed nave windows with hoodmoulds on square stops are early 16th century. There is a monument to Reynald Portrey, d1629.

PORT TALBOT   *St Mary*
SS 763902

Pritchard & Seddon's church of 1858-9 contains an altar table dated 1704 in the south aisle, whilst the north aisle has one reset window from a previous church on this site.

Pyle Church

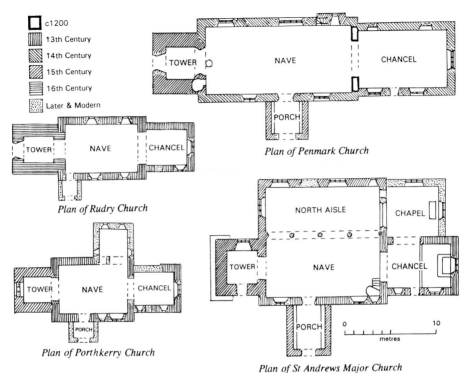

Legend:
- c1200
- 13th Century
- 14th Century
- 15th Century
- 16th Century
- Later & Modern

Plan of Penmark Church

Plan of Rudry Church

Plan of Porthkerry Church

Plan of St Andrews Major Church

PYLE   *St James*   SS 825826

One of the shields on the wall-plate of the wagon roof bears the date 1471. The whole church is thought to have been erected then to replace a church at Kenfig engulfed by shifting sand dunes. Comparatively little restored, it comprises a west tower with a stair projection on the south side, a nave with two-light south windows with hoodmoulds, a chancel and a south porch. The octagonal font with roundels and trees is of the same period. There is a tablet to Edward Thomas, d1693.

RADYR   *St John the Baptist*   St 133802

The church has been mostly rebuilt but has an old font and chancel arch.

RUDRY   *St Augustine*   ST 194865

The saddleback-roofed west tower has a round-arched west doorway. The nave and chancel are old but the only medieval features are traces of a priest's doorway on the south side and of a roodloft stair doorway on the north, and perhaps the font.

RUMNEY   *St Augustine*   ST 215791

The very long nave has a battered base to the north wall, perhaps of c1200 since a doorway of that period with shafts and a keeled roll on the arch has been reset in the west tower. Of the 15th century are the chancel arch and priest's doorway, the octagonal font bowl on a stem with spurs, the outer arch of the porch, and the upper parts (at least) of the tower with short crocketed pinnacles and battlements.

St Athan Church

Tomb slab at St Bride's Major

ST ANDREWS MAJOR   *St Andrew*   ST 138715

The high west tower with a corbelled parapet and a south doorway, the porch and the wide north aisle date from a remodelling of c1480-1520. The aisle has a four bay arcade with octagonal piers without capitals. At the east end an arch leads into a north chapel rebuilt in 1921 which now serves as a vestry. The nave and chancel may be 13th century (the possible date of the south doorway) and the font is Norman. The chancel arch and east window date from a restoration of 1875-9.

ST ATHAN   *St Tathan*   ST 017680

This is a cruciform church with the row of four restored late 13th century lancets in the chancel south wall as its earliest features. The nave west window is mid 14th century and about that time the south transept was provided with a squint, a crocketed piscina, a square-headed three-light east window with reticulated tracery, and the splendid ogival-arched recess in the south wall to contain the effigies of Sir Roger Berkerolles, d1351, and his wife, whose seat was East Orchard Manor, perched above the River Thaw to the east. The effigies of Sir Roger's father St William, d1327, and mother are later (not earlier) in date and more damaged. Of the 15th century are the south porch, central tower, and the wagon roofs. The Y-traceried windows in the nave and the north transept windows are of 1888.

ST BRIDES MAJOR   *St Bridget*   SS 894750

The porch and nave windows date from the drastic restoration of 1851 but the masonry may be partly Norman since there is a chancel arch of that period. The chancel has a 14th century east window and north and south lancets with ogival heads. Of the 15th century are the font and the west tower with a corbelled parapet, diagonal buttresses, corner pinnacles projecting on heads and a SE stair turret with cross-loops with oillets. The small early 16th century figure of a martyred saint is assumed to be St Bridget. Under the altar is an incised slab depicting John Butler (or Botiler), c1340, and there is a tomb chest in the chancel north wall with a cross-legged effigy of John Butler, d1540, lying beside his wife. There are several 17th century tablets and also busts of John Wyndham, d1697, and his wife.

ST BRIDES MINOR   *St Bride*   SS 896835

G.E.Halliday added a north aisle in 1896. In the nave his restoration has left a niche south of the chancel arch as the only ancient feature. The chancel arch itself, the priest's doorway and one chancel south window are 14th or 15th century.

ST BRIDES-SUPER-ELY   *St Bride*   ST 097776

The saddleback-roofed west tower with trefoil-headed belfry windows is probably late 13th century. The nave south doorway is Norman and has scales in spandrels under a gable. The Norman chancel arch has been renewed, and another Norman arch with chevrons in the outer porch entrance has come from Margam. The east window is another import, from a former chapel of St Mary at Sant-y-Nyll not far to the north. Its centre light is filled with a vaulted 15th century image niche. The window contains imported stained glass and a 15th century fragment showing an angel.

St Bride's-super-Ely Church   *St Brides Major Church*

ST DONATS   *St Donat*   SS 933681

The church lies deep in a valley below the castle. The chancel arch and font are Norman. The west tower is probably early 14th century and the north chapel with a square-headed east window of three lights with reticulated tracery is late 14th century. In the 15th century the chancel was rebuilt, and the nave remodelled with a new south wall with three-light windows, and a new doorway and porch and roodloft staircase on the north, whilst both nave and tower were embattled, with gargoyles on the nave and corbelling on the tower. The rare painted panels of the 1590s showing members of the Stradling family are no longer in the church, although they were recovered after being stolen in 1991. In the chapel are effigies of Sir Edward, d1609, and his wife, and a monument to the last two Stradlings, Sir Edward, d1726, and Sir Thomas, d1738. There is a fine churchyard cross (see page 6.)

ST FAGANS   *St Mary*   ST 122772

The nave south wall contains traces of two Norman windows. Otherwise the nave and chancel are fine 14th century work with triple sedilia and a piscina in the chancel, where there are two light windows with hoodmoulds on dragons or heads on each side and a three light east window. The wide north aisle and north vestry were added during a restoration by G.E.Street in 1859-60, and there is much late 19th century stained glass. The tower is dated 1730 on the west side, although it is mostly probably about a century older than that, and the tower arch is 14th century. The 15th century font has quatrefoils and a panelled stem.

ST GEORGES   *St George*   ST 105766

The lack of any north windows suggests an early date for the nave. In the 14th century the church was made cruciform with the addition of transepts and a new chancel, although above the crossing (with the arms of Iestyn ap Gwrgant on the boss of the vault) the existing central tower with a four-gabled top dates from 1838, when the north transept was also rebuilt. There are two tomb recesses of differing sizes in the chancel, and old wagon roofs remain in the nave and south transept. The octagonal font with quatrefoils in circles is 15th century. The oldest monument is a tablet with an urn to John Llewellin, d1786.

St Fagans Church

St Georges Church

St Lythans Church

St Donats Church

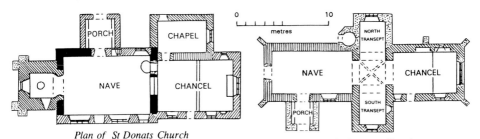

Plan of St Donats Church

Plan of St Georges Church

ST HILARY   *St Hilary*   ST 016733

The plain pointed chancel arch and the reset south doorway are of c1200 but the priest's doorway looks a century older. The ogival headed lancet in the chancel north wall looks like a Norman opening modified later. The four-bay south arcade and tower arch are 14th century but the diagonally buttressed tower itself is of c1500, whilst the aisle was mostly rebuilt in 1861-2, when the chancel was given two new windows and the nave north wall another one. No furnishings survived the restoration but there are effigies of Thomas Basset, d1423, and of a 14th century man of the de Cardiff family in civilian dress. Only the steps remain of a churchyard cross. See p8.

ST LYTHANS   *St Bleiddian*   ST 111729

The font with six rows of chevrons is Norman, and the saddleback-roofed tower, nave and chancel all probably have 13th century masonry. The porch is of the 1860s, and all the windows have been restored but those on the south were 15th century. The square 16th century chapel on the south side has a very rustic-looking two-bay arcade and a west doorway with initials of Robert Button of Dyffryn House.

ST MARY CHURCH   *St Mary*   ST 002716

The church was mostly rebuilt by Pritchard & Seddon in 1862, but there remain a tub font, a pillar piscina with a twisted stem, an embattled tower, and both nave and chancel still have medieval roofs, the latter with a celure over the altar.

ST MARY HILL   *St Mary*   SS 957793

The former Norman chancel arch now forms a rere-arch to one of the nave north windows. The chancel has an ogival-headed aumbry with a carved head, and the priest's doorway and font are old, but otherwise the church was mostly rebuilt in 1879-81. The most notable of the collection of 17th and 18th century tablets are those to two successive Watkin Hopkins, who died in 1699 and 1702.

ST MELLONS   *St Mellon*   ST 228814

The small chancel and the long, wide nave have their south walls in line with each other, suggesting that the nave has been widened. The 13th century tower with a 15th century top lies in the middle of the south side. West of it is a big porch and east of it is a 14th century chapel with an arcade of two bays towards the nave and a third arch towards the chancel. The 15th century windows of the chapel are renewed. The north chapel is probably 17th century. The font with a panelled stem is probably 15th century, as are the benches with poppyheads in the nave.

ST NICHOLAS   *St Nicholas*   ST 090744

The tower arch and chancel are early 14th century, and the south doorway and porch could also be of that period. The font and the nave windows are 15th century, although two windows on the north are renewed. The large south chapel extending from the porch east wall (in which are blocked windows) to the chancel east wall has a south wall of 1893 and windows of 1860, but the arch between it and the nave looks early 16th century.

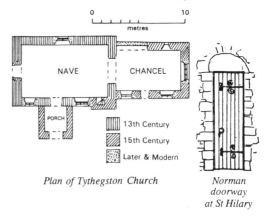

Plan of Tythegston Church

Norman doorway at St Hilary

St Nicholas Church

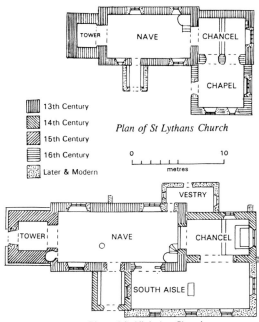

13th Century
14th Century
15th Century
16th Century
Later & Modern

Plan of St Lythans Church

0   10
metres

Plan of St Nicholas Church

St Mellons Church

SULLY   *St John the Baptist*   ST 152684

A Norman chancel arch and a 15th century south aisle and porch are said to have been removed in the early 19th century. If so the three-light 15th century south windows much be reset, whilst the north windows are of 1927. The rendered nave now contains no doorway and entrance is by a doorway dated 1701 in the tower south wall. The chancel has a 13th century trefoil-headed piscina and a window and priest's doorway of the 15th century. The small wooden font may be 18th century, but there is a larger and grander font of c1850.

TALYGARN   *St Anne*   ST 026802

The existing church was built in 1887 at the expense of G.T.Clark, industrialist and author of Medieval Military Architecture in England. The older chapel lying in ruins beside it with large segmental-headed south windows is said to be mostly of the time of a rebuilding in 1687 for Sir Leoline Jenkins.

TYTHEGSTON   *St Tydwg*   SS 858788

The west doorway, porch and chancel features are of c1450-1520, but the nave doorway and font are probably older and a former north chapel has been removed. The building was heavily restored by Pritchard in 1876.

VAYNOR   *St Gwynno*   SO 049104

Near the church of 1870 is a ruinous small single chamber medieval church with a small 16th century tower inserted into the west end of it.

Welsh St Donats Church

WELSH ST DONATS   *St Donat*   ST 027763

The circular font with scallops under the bowl is 13th century and the nave and chancel with a plain pointed arch between them are probably of that date. Several two-light windows with square hoodmoulds and the arched braced roofs of the nave and chancel are early 16th century and the tower top and west doorway are also of that period, although the tower base is probably older.

WENVOE   *St Mary*   ST 123726

The church was much restored in 1876 and has a north vestry of 1930 lying where there was a tower until a new one was built at the west end in 1699. The north transept was added as recently as 1989-91. Inside are three fine monuments to owners of Wenvoe Castle: William Thomas, d1636, Sir John Thomas, d1704, and his wife, and Peter Birt, d1791.

WEST ABERTHAW   *Dedication Unknown*   ST 024667

In the 1980s a cattle shed here was revealed to be a much altered medieval chapel still retaining two blocked windows and a piscina.

WHITCHURCH   *St Mary*   ST 155804

In St Mary's Gardens, Old Church Road, 0.4km east of Pritchard's new church of 1882-4 with a porch-tower, lie the lower parts of the nave, south porch and square chancel of a medieval church demolished in 1904.

WICK   *St James*   SS 924722

The nave rebuilt by Pritchard in 1871 was originally Norman like the font with a rope-moulding, and the chancel arch, plus one south window in the chancel. The two image niches in the chancel east wall may be 15th century. The west tower has a saddleback roof. The oldest monument is that of Elizabeth Lloyd, d1723.

BACKINSTON   *Dedication Unknown*   SS 576881

In a field is the ivy-mantled ruin of a tiny chapel just 5.6m long by 3.6m wide externally. The doorway is the only surviving feature.

Backinston Chapel

BISHOPSTON   *St Teilo*   SS 578893

The chancel with single and paired lancets is 13th century, and so probably is the embattled and corbelled west tower. The nave could be earlier but one 15th century window is the earliest feature. The roof is partly old but the porch and other windows are 19th century. There is also an ancient font.

BURRY HOLMS   *St Cennyd*   SS 401926

On an island beyond Llangenneth Burrows are the remains of a small Norman chapel, once part of a hermitage with buildings of various periods. The tiny square chancel has replaced a former apse. Excavations in the 1960s found traces of a wooden Early Christian period chapel and burials of a still older period.

CASWELL   *St Peter*   SS 590883

The east gable of a chapel with the outline of a large window and foundations of the side walls lie hidden under foliage in a valley near Bishopston.

CHERITON   *St Cadoc*   ST 450932

This is a comparatively unaltered 13th century church comprising a nave, central tower and a square chancel. Original are several lancets and the fine south doorway with a hood with three rolls, and one order of columns with shaft-rings and stiff-leaf capitals. The nave has an old wagon roof. The tower has a gabled roof within a corbelled parapet. The south porch and the north transeptal vestry are of 1874.

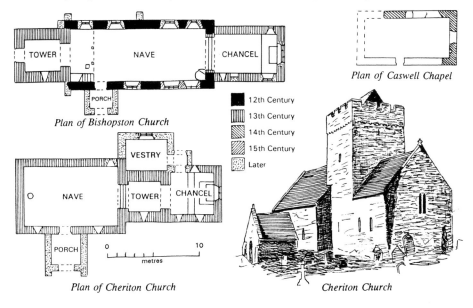

Plan of Bishopston Church

Plan of Caswell Chapel

- ■ 12th Century
- ▥ 13th Century
- ▨ 14th Century
- ▧ 15th Century
- ▦ Later

Plan of Cheriton Church

Cheriton Church

CWRT-Y-CARNE   *St Michael*   SN 573004

Little remains of this chapel in marshland beside the Loughor estuary. It was a grange of Neath Abbey and was probably 12th or 13th century with a later porch. The ruined walls were still almost intact as late as 1899.

ILSTON   *ST Illtyd*   SS 557904

The church is picturesquely situated by a stream in a valley and it whitewashed throughout inside. The nave is probably Norman and the two doorways (one is blocked) could be original. Neither the chancel with its axis rather to the south of that of the nave nor the irregularly position south transeptal tower with a saddleback roof with battlements on the east and west sides only can be securely dated, but they are probably 13th century. A south chapel has been rebuilt to serve as a vestry and the east window and south porch are also mid 19th century. The chancel has a tomb recess on the north side. The only monument of note is to James Mansel, d1769. Amongst the woods in Ilstom Cwm (at SS 553894) are slight remains of the well chapel of St Cenydd. From 1649 until 1660 the then vicar, John Myles, used the chapel, for Baptist services, making this the first Baptist chapel in Wales.

KNELSTON   *St Mary*   SS 468890

Beyond a farm near Knelston School are footings of a small medieval chapel which was already ruinous by 1688.

LLANDDEWI   *St David*   SS 460890

The saddleback-roofed west tower with corbelling to the east and west, and the chancel with one north lancet, are 13th century additions to a Norman nave retaining on north window and a tub font of that period. The porch may be 13th century and the window east of it is 14th century, as is the blocked window in the chancel north wall. Three other windows are of the restorations of 1876 and 1905. There are 18th century altar rails with twisted balusters.

LLANDEILO TAL-Y-BONT   *St Teilo*   SN 585030

Little remains on the site since the ruin has been removed for eventual reconstruction at the St Fagans Welsh Folk Museum. It comprised a 13th or 14th century nave and chancel to which a south aisle and porch and a north chapel were added in the 15th century. The east wall was later rebuilt and new side windows provided. In the 1980s wall paintings of c1500 with various saints were discovered.

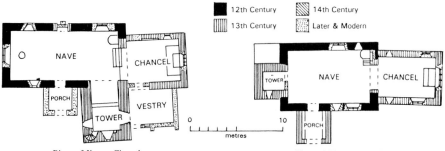

■ 12th Century   ▧ 14th Century
▥ 13th Century   ▦ Later & Modern

Plan of Ilston Church   *Plan of Llanddewi Church*

Llangennith Church

Ilston Church

LLANGENNITH *St Cenydd* SS 428914

The north transeptal tower has paired lancets and a saddleback roof with corbelled parapets to the north and south. It looks 13th century, as does the nave north doorway, but the blocked round headed east arch to a former chapel or apse suggests the lower part may be Norman. Of the 14th century are the east window of the long chancel and the effigy of one of the De la Mares. The other windows and perhaps the chancel arch are of 1882. On the west wall is a fragment of a 9th century cross-shaft with interlace. There is a tablet to Richard Portrey, d1715.

Llandeilo Tal-Y-Bont Church

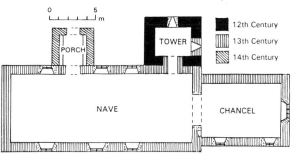

0   5
m

■ 12th Century
▨ 13th Century
▨ 14th Century

TOWER

PORCH

NAVE

CHANCEL

Plan of Llangennith Church

Tower arch at Llangyfelach   *Llanrhidian Church*

LLANGYFELACH   *St Cyfelach*   SS 646990

Only the embattled tower with a plain pointed arch remains of the medieval church, the rest of which was demolished after suffering storm damage in 1803. The existing church not far below to the north has a nave which is said to have originally been a barn. A chancel was added to it in 1850 and the nave was made more church-like in 1913-14. A fragment of a Celtic cross-shaft is set in its north wall, and other (now very worn) lies over the doorway on the north side of the old tower. In the new church are monuments to Thomas Price, d1754, Jane Price, d1758, and Mary Price, d1782. There is also a brass depicting Mathew Johnes and his wife, d1631.

LLANMADOC   *St Madoc*   SS 439935

The nave and chancel were Norman until mostly rebuilt in 1865-6. Of that date is the saddleback roofed top of the tiny west tower. A 5th or 6th century stone set into a nave south window is inscribed Guan, son of Advectus, lies here. At the west end are two stones inscribed with crosses, 7th to 9th century.

LLANRHIDIAN   *St Rhidian & St Illtyd*   SS 496922

The chancel has 15th century windows and the large west tower with a vaulted lower stage and a SE stair turret is also of that period. The nave and porch were rebuilt in 1856-8. In the porch is a 9th or 10th century lintel stone with animals and figures thought to depict St Paul and St Anthony meeting in the desert.

LOUGHOR   *St Michael*   SS 564980

The nave and chancel were rebuilt on the old foundations in 1885 and then provided with a large bellcote. Only the monument to Hannah Williams, d1706, is older.

NICHOLASTON   *St Nicholas*   SS 513884

The church was rebuilt in 1892-4 for Miss Olive Talbot except for the chancel arch and font. Although small it has many fancy details mostly in 13th century style.

Oxwich Church

Plan of Oxwich Church

Oystermouth Church

OXWICH *St Illtyd* SS 505861

The more thickly walled eastern half of the nave and the very tiny chancel formed a Norman chapel. The nave was doubled in length in the 14th century, when a west tower was added and the chancel given a new east window and a ogival-headed tomb recess on the north side in which are effigies of one of the Penrice family and his wife. The square-headed windows in the nave are of c1500.

OYSTERMOUTH *All Saints* SS 616880

The west tower with a south stair turret, the long nave, and the chancel with triple east lancets and a pillar piscina are all probably 13th century, although the tower top, screen, and several windows are late medieval. The medieval part now forms a south aisle to a new church of 1915-6 on the site of a north aisle added in 1857-60, of which the arcade remains. There is a fine 13th century font with scallops under the square bowl. The church is thought to lie on the site of a Roman villa.

Llanmadoc Church

PENCLAWDD   *St Gwynour*   SS 549949

The octagonal font is the only relic of the medieval church. The nave and tower (with a rebuilt spire) are of 1850 and the chancel, vestry and organ chamber are of 1926.

PENMAEN   *St John the Baptist*   SS 532887 & 532882

The foundations of the original Norman nave and chancel church out amongst the dunes were excavated in 1860 but are now hard to find. The existing church, probably of 14th century origin, was mostly rebuilt in 1854. One grave slabs, one of 1675, are the only pre-Victorian features of interest.

PENNARD   *St Mary*   SS 545855 & 566887

Near the castle is a defaced fragment and foundations of the Norman church engulfed by sand in the 14th century, when the present church further east was built to replace it. The new building is almost the same size as the older one and incorporates the chancel arch and two lancets from the older building. The porch and diminutive tower set upon a thickened west wall are 15th century. The north transept and vestry are 19th century, as are the nave windows with Y-tracery, but the east window is of c1500. The font has been assembled from old parts and has a 17th century cover. The 17th century pulpit (see page 11) has come from an Oxfordshire church. There are also Royal Arms and altar rails with turned balusters, probably both 18th century.

PENRICE   *St Andrew*   SS 493879

The nave is Norman and is divided from the rebuilt chancel by an round arch with an angle roll. The embattled and corbelled west tower is probably 13th century. Flanking the nave, but set back from its east end, are what look like transepts. The southern one serves as a porch, with seats on each side, a moulded and filleted outer arch of c1300 and an inner doorway of formed from three massive timbers, whilst the northern one is partitioned to form a baptistry and vestry. The nave windows were renewed in the restoration of 1893-4. There are monuments to ten week old John Hancorne, d1746, and (of 1726) to the Bennet family.

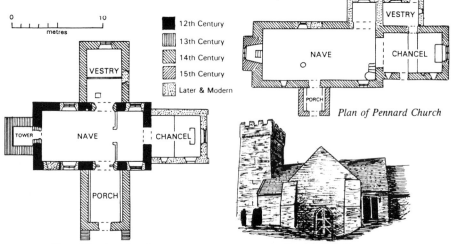

0   metres   10

■ 12th Century
▨ 13th Century
▧ 14th Century
▨ 15th Century
▦ Later & Modern

VESTRY

NAVE   CHANCEL

PORCH

Plan of Pennard Church

TOWER   NAVE   CHANCEL

PORCH

Plan of Penrice Church

Penrice Church

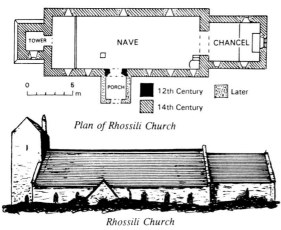

Plan of Rhossili Church

Rhossili Church

Pennard Church

PORT EYNON   *St Catwg*   SS 466854

The chancel contains one blocked ogival-headed lancet and the nave has a round-headed south doorway probably of the 16th century, but both parts and the small north transept were mostly rebuilt in 1861. There are no east or west windows. The square font on a spurred quatrefoil stem is 13th century. Over the pulpit is a 16th century shield with the arms and initials of Rice Mansel.

REYNOLDSTON   *St George*   SS 479900

Only a medieval font and a reset Norman window on the south side have survived the rebuilding of 1866-7. There are also a 9th century stone with an incised cross on one side and interlace on the other, and a tablet to John Lucas, d1787.

RHOSSILI   *St Mary*   SS 417881 & 414883

The original Norman church lower down the slope was dug out of the dunes which had engulfed it in 1980. Simple painted patterns were found on the walls, which remained almost complete. The long, low 14th century church with a saddleback-roofed west tower in the middle of the village has a fine Late Norman south doorway with one order of columns which must have been the chancel arch of the original church. The chancel has an original trefoil-headed recess but the windows are all of 1855 or 1890. The font must also go back to the time of the original church.

SWANSEA   *St Mary*   SS 656929

The only medieval relics now are a fragment of an effigy of a 14th century lady and a fine brass of c1500 depicting Sir Hugh Johnys of Landimore and his wife Maude. The medieval nave was rebuilt in 1739, but the whole building was rebuilt in 1894-8. Further rebuilding in the 1950s was necessitated by wartime bombing in which the fine ornamental tomb of Sir Matthew Craddock was destroyed along with the Herbert Chapel. The result is a building with wide aisles, transepts and a south tower.

A second medieval church dedicated to St John by the northern part of the High Street outside the town walls has gone. The church of St Matthew of 1823-4, but remodelled and extended in 1885-6, stands on the site.

GLOSSARY OF TERMS

Apse	-	Semi-circular or polygonal east end of a church containing an altar.
Ashlar	-	Masonry of blocks with even faces and square edges.
Broaches	-	Sloping half pyramids adapting an octagonal spire to a square tower.
Chancel	-	The eastern part of a church used by the clergy.
Chevron Ornament	-	A continuous series of Vs forming a zig-zag.
Clerestory	-	The upper part of the nave of a church, pierced by windows.
Collar Beam	-	A tie-beam used higher up nearer the apex of a roof.
Corbel	-	A projecting bracket supporting a wall, image or beam.
Corbel Table	-	A continuous row of corbels supporting a parapet.
Crossing Tower	-	A tower built upon four arches in the middle of a cruciform church.
Cusp	-	A projecting point between the foils of a Gothic arch.
Decorated	-	A division of English Gothic architecture roughly from 1290 to 1360.
Dog-tooth	-	Four cornered star placed diagonally and raised pyramidally.
Early English	-	The first division of English Gothic architecture from c1200 to 1290.
Elizabethan	-	Of the time of the reign of Queen Elizabeth I (1558-1603).
Embattled	-	Provided with a series of indentations (crenels).
Fleuron	-	Rectilinear flower or leaf carved in low relief.
Foil	-	A lobe formed by the cusping of a circle or an arch.
Four Centred Arch	-	A low, pointed arch with each curve drawn from two compass points.
Hagioscope	-	(or Squint) A hole cut in a wall to allow a view of the high altar.
Head Stops	-	Heads of humans or beasts forming the ends of a hoodmould.
Herringbone Masonry	-	Courses of stones alternately sloping at 45 degrees to horizontal.
Hoodmould	-	A projecting moulding above a doorway or window to throw off water.
Impost	-	A wall bracket, often moulded, to support the end of an arch.
Jacobean	-	Of the time of the reign of James I (1603-25).
Jamb	-	The side of a doorway, window or other opening.
Lancet	-	A long, comparatively narrow window usually with a pointed head.
Light	-	A compartment of a window.
Misericord	-	Bracket underneath hinged choir stall seat to support standing person.
Mullion	-	A vertical member dividing the lights of a window.
Nave	-	The part of a church in which the congregation sits (or stood originally).
Norman	-	Division of English Romanesque architecture from 1066 to c1200.
Ogival Arch	-	Arch of oriental origin with both convex and concave curves.
Perpendicular	-	A division of English Gothic architecture from c1360 to 1540.
Pilaster	-	Flat buttress or pier attached to a wall. Used in the Norman period.
Piscina	-	A stone basin used for rinsing out holy vessels after mass.
Plinth	-	The projecting base of a wall.
Quoins	-	Dressed or cut stones used at the corners of a building.
Rere-Arch	-	The arch over the inner opening of a doorway or window embrasure.
Respond	-	A half-pier or column bonded into a wall to carry one end of an arch.
Reticulation	-	Tracery with a netlike appearance. Current c1320-70.
Rood Loft	-	Loft over screen between nave and chancel with crucifix (rood) upon it.
Sedilia	-	Seats for priests (usually three) on the south side of a chancel.
Soffit	-	The underside of an arch or lintel.
Spandrel	-	The surface between two arches or a wall and an arch.
Tie-Beam	-	A beam connecting the slopes of a roof at or near its foot.
Tracery	-	The intersecting ribwork in the upper part of a later Gothic window.
Transept	-	A chamber containing a side altar on the north or south side of a church.
Tympanum	-	A space between a lintel of a doorway and an arch above it.
Wall-Plate	-	A timber laid longitudinally along the top of a wall.
Windbraces	-	The struts used to strengthen the sloping sides of a roof.

FURTHER READING

Buildings of Wales: Glamorgan (1995) & Gwent (2000) vols, both by John Newman.
Medieval Churches of the Vale of Glamorgan, Geoffrey Orrin, 1988.
Lost Churches of Wales and the Marches, Paul R.Davis & Susan Lloyd Fern, 1990.
Periodicals: Morgannwg, Gwent Local History, Archeologia Cambrensis.